HISTORICALLY

BLACK COLLEGES

AND

UNIVERSITIES

WHAT YOU SHOUD KNOW

ALPHONSO W. KNIGHT SR.

Copyright © 2017 by ALPHONSO W. KNIGHT SR.

All rights reserved. This book or any portion thereof may not be reproduced or transmitted in any form or manner, electronic or mechanical, including photocopying, recording, or by any information storage or retrieval system, without the express written permission of the copyright owner except for the use of brief quotations in a book review or other noncommercial uses permitted by copyright law.

Printed in the United States of America

Library of Congress Control Number: 2017962452

ISBN: Hardcover: 978-1-948304-14-6

               Softcover: 978-1-948304-25-2

               ePub: 978-1-948304-13-9

Rev.date:12/04/2017

To order copies of this book, contact:

PageTurner, Press and Media
601 E., Palomar St., Suite C-478, Chula Vista, CA 91911
Phone: 1-888-447-9651
Fax: 1-619-632-6328
www.pageturner.us

TABLE OF CONTENTS

PREFACE

In presenting this information on historically black colleges and universities, the author found in his contact and travels that a large number of blacks are unaware of the existence of historically black colleges and universities in America, where they are located and the contributions these schools have and are making in higher education today. More disturbing is the lack of knowledge among a great number of non-blacks and the public in general of the existence of these schools. It is, therefore, necessary to inform these individuals about these institutions that comprise the historically black colleges and about their contributions.

Historical black colleges and universities as defined by the Black College and University Act are those institutions that were established prior to 1964 with the goal to educate black Americans. The role of these institutions has been a constant or recurrent debate within the framework of higher education since legal racial segregation in the United States of America has existed. The primary purpose of the historically black colleges was to educate black Americans. This was done practically exclusively from 1865 to the 1950s. The majority of historically black colleges and universities opened their doors after 1865 in response to the need to have institutions to educate newly freed slaves and to avoid admitting these newly freed slaves into the existing white institutions.

It has been documented that only about 20% of African Americans attend historically black colleges while 80% of African Americans attend predominantly white colleges and universities in the United States. Research reveals that those blacks finishing in predominantly white schools are offered and end up getting more lucrative and prestigious positions in the corporate and industrial worlds as opposed to blacks who finish from historically black schools.

HBCUs is the acronym for historically black colleges and universities and is most often used in describing African American schools.

Research has listed 105 historical black colleges and universities in the United States today, including public and private, two-year and four-year institutions, medical schools and community colleges. Most of these are or were in the former slave states and territories of the United States. Exceptions are Central State University (Ohio), Cheyney University (Pennsylvania), Lincoln University (Pennsylvania), Wilberforce University (Ohio), Lewis College of Business (Michigan) and Western University (Kansas). Some of these schools which operated for decades closed during the 20th Century due to competition, the Great Depression and financial difficulties.

The Higher Education Act of 1965 was amended and defines a "part B institution" as any historically black college or university that was established prior to 1964, whose principle mission was and is , the education of black Americans, and is accredited by a national accrediting agency or association determined by the Secretary of Education to be a reliable authority as to the quality of training offered or is, according to such an agency or association, making reasonable progress toward accreditation. Part B of the 1965 Act provides for direct aid to Part B institutions.

In 1863, the Morrill Act provided for land grant colleges in each state. Some educational institutions in the North and West were opened to blacks since the Civil War. However, 17 Southern states generally excluded blacks from the land grant colleges. In response, the second Morrill Act of 1890 was passed to require states to establish a separate land grant college for blacks if blacks were being excluded from the then existing land grant colleges. Many of the HBCUs were founded in response to the second Morrill Act. These land grant schools continue to receive annual federal funding for their research, extension and outreach activities. In 1965, the Higher Education Act established a program for direct federal grants to HBCUs, including federal matching of private endowment contributions. To note, there are 103 HBCUs that are located mainly in the Southeastern, South-Midwestern, the District of Columbia and the Virgin Islands of the United States.

Other educational institutions have large members of blacks in their student body as they opened their doors to African Americans after the implementation of the Sweatt V. Painter and Brown versus Board of Education rulings by the U. S. Supreme Court (the court decisions which outlawed racial segregation of public education facilities) and the Higher

Education Act of 1965. They are not historically black colleges, but have been termed "predominantly black".

In 2001, libraries of several HBCUs began conversation about ways to pool their resources and work collaboratively. In 2003, this partnering was formalized as the HBCU Library Alliance, a "consortium that supports the collaboration of information professionals dedicated to providing an array of resources designed to strengthen HBCUs and their constituents".

Research reveals that of the 105 HBCU institutions in America today, 27 offer doctoral programs and 52 offer graduate degree programs at the Master's level, 83 offer a Bachelor's degree program and 38 of the schools provide associate degrees. The number of Bachelor degrees awarded to black students by HBCUs has steadily dropped from 35% in 1976 to 21.5% in 2001. From 1976 to 2001, total HBCU enrollment grew from 180,059 to 222,453, with most of the increase being attributed to the growth of black female enrollment from 88,379 to 117,766.

In 2004, the U. S. Department of Education published a study of HBCUs that found that, as of 2001, HBCUs accounted for 13% of black higher education enrollment. In 2007, the Thurgood Marshall Fund published a study of minority recruiting practices by Fortune 400 companies and by government agencies that found that 13% of the college graduates were recruited from HBCUs and 87% were recruited from non-HBCUs schools.

Following the enactment of Civil Rights laws in the 1960s, all educational institutions that received federal funding have undertaken affirmative action to increase their racial diversity. Some historical black colleges now have non-black majorities, notably West Virginia State University, Kentucky State University and Bluefield State College whose student body has been roughly 90% white since the mid-1960s. Many non-state-supported HBCUs are struggling financially, due to increased cost of delivering private education to students and declining financial aid for students. As colleges work harder to maintain enrollment levels, the percentage of non-African American enrollment has tended to climb.

Conclusion: The environment existing at the historically black school offers a uniqueness of individual and group binding in social and economic perception of living and working which is absent to a great degree at the predominant white school for the black student. This condition impacts on job availability in the work world for the black graduate from a predominant black school.

The publishing of this information in this book concerning HBCUs is to enlighten those who are unaware of the existence of these schools and the important role these schools have played and are playing in the education of African Americans and others in the total higher education picture in the United States today. It is hoped that the knowledge of their existence will inspire African Americans, as well as others, to examine the need for attending and supporting these institutions.

Furthermore, this publication is dedicated to those African Americans and others who see the need to take advantage of the existence of these HBCUs to educate themselves to gain an opportunity in preparing for a productive life which was and has denied them under the laws of slavery. Furthermore, it serves as a reminder that the existence of HBCUs are still vitally important in providing education for those who have difficulty in entering some of the long-standing predominant white schools. It presents all of the HBCUs under one roof, providing information on the school's history, establishment, type, location, phone, religious affiliation, student enrollment, tuition/fees, academic staff, campus type and size, school colors, nickname, athletic and sports affiliation, endowment and notable alumni. It provides the interested individual needed and readied facts for comparison and for arriving at a decision on the school of one's choice as opposed to the time involved in seeking information collectively from each institution through mailing and visiting each institution.

This publication also provides needed information for aspiring high school students, high school guidance counselors, high school teachers, college admission counselors, college and high school libraries and alumni recruitment officials. It is hoped that the information this book provides will be valuable to those blacks and others who yearn for more information on black colleges and universities.

MORRILL LAND-GRANT ACTS:

The Morrill Land-Grant Acts are United States statuses that allowed for the creation of land-grant colleges, including the Morrill Acts of 1862 and 1890. The Morrill Acts funded educational institution in the United States designated by a state to receive the benefits of the Morrill Acts of 1862 and 1890. The Morrill Acts funded educational institutions by granting federal controlled land to the states for them to establish and endow "land-grant" colleges. The mission of these institutions as set forth in the 1962 Act is to focus on the teaching of practical agriculture, science, military science and engineering, as a response to the industrial revolution and changing social class. Ultimately, most land-grant colleges became large public universities that now offer a full spectrum of educational opportunities.

Under provision six of the Act, "No state while in a condition of rebellion or insurrection against the government of the United States shall be entitled to the benefit of the Act," in reference to secession of several Southern states and the raging of the Civil War. After the war, however, the 1862 Act was extended to the former Confederate states; it was eventually extended to every state and territory, included those created after 1862.

A second Morrill Act in 1890 was also aimed at the former Confederate states. This act required each state to show that race was not an admission criterion, or else to designate a separate land-grant institution of color. Among the seventy colleges and universities which eventually evolved from the Morrill Acts are several of today's HBCUs. Though the 1890 Act granted cash instead of land, it granted colleges under the act the same legal standing as the 1862 Act colleges; hence the term "land grant college" properly applies to both groups. Later on, other colleges such as the University of the District of Columbia and the "1994 land-grant colleges" for Native Americans were also awarded cash by Congress in lieu of land to achieve "land-grant" status.

THURGOOD MARSHALL COLLEGE FUND:

The Thurgood Marshall College Fund (TMCF) is a philanthropic organization that fund raises college tuition funds for black students and general scholarship funds for 54 schools. The Fund was established in 1987 to carry on Justice Thurgood Marshall's legacy of ensuring equal access to higher education by supporting exceptional scholars attending America's public historically black colleges and universities as well as six law schools which historically taught black students. This contrasts with the United Negro College Fund which is directed toward private colleges. The fund was renamed the Thurgood Marshall College Fund in 2006. The Fund has since expanded to include medical schools. TMCF has awarded more than $100 million in scholarships and programmatic support during its history. It has a partnership with the Lilly Endowment Inc. which funded the training of over 600 Developmental executives at the Indiana University

Center on Philanthropy.

In 2003, five of its member universities and Bill and Melinda Gates Foundation partnered to form education at six high schools in rural and urban communities in Louisiana, Maryland, North Carolina and Texas.

In 2007, the TMCF funded a study of minority recruiting by Fortune 400 companies and by government agencies that found that 13% of the college graduates were recruited from HBUCs and 87% were recruited from non-HBCU schools.

UNITED NEGRO COLLEGE FUND:

The United Negro College Fund (UNCF) is an American philanthropic organization that funds scholarships for black students and general scholarship funds for 39 private historically black colleges and universities. The UNCF was incorporated on April 25, 1944 by Frederick D. Patterson, (then president of Tuskegee Institute), Mary McLeod Bethune, former president of Behtune-Cookman College and other. In 2005, the UNCF supported approximately 65,000 students at over 900 colleges and universities with approximately $113 million in grants and scholarships. Approximately 80% of these students are the first in their family to attend college, and 62% have annual family incomes of less than $25,000. UNCF also administers over 450 named scholarships. This fund contrasts with the Thurgood Marshall Fund that raises money for public historically black colleges and universities.

Location of UNCF member institutions: Alabama, Arkansas, Ethiopia, Florida, Georgia, Louisiana, Mississippi, North Carolina, Ohio, South Carolina, Tennessee, Texas, and Virginia. The headquarters for the UNCF is 8260 Willow Oaks Corporate Dr., Fairfax, Va. 22031.

DEFUNCT HBCUS

Bishop College - located in Dallas, TX, founded in 1881, private affiliated with the African Episcopal Methodist Church, closed in 1975.

Daniel Payne College - located in Birmingham, AL, founded in 1889, private, affiliated with AME Church, closed in 1979.

Friendship College - located in Rock Hill, S.C., founded in 1891, private, affiliated with the Baptist Church, closed in 1981.

Guadalupe College - located in Seguin, TX, founded in 1884, private, affiliated with Texas Missionary Baptist General Convention, closed in 1936.

Kittrell College - located in Kittrell, N.C., founded in 1886, private, affiliated with the African Episcopal Methodist Church, closed in 1975.

Leland University - located in New Orleans, LA, private, affiliated with Home Mission Society, closed in the 1970s.

Mary Holmes College - located in West Point, MS, founded in 1892, private, affiliated with American Missionary Association, closed in 1993.

Natchez College - located in Natchez, MS, founded in 1885, private, affiliated with the Baptist Church, closed in 1993.

Saint Paul's College - located in Lawrenceville, VA, founded in 1865, private, affiliated with Freewill Baptist Missionary Society, closed in 2013.

Roger Williams College - located in Nashville, TN, founded in 1864, private, affiliated with the Home Mission Society, closed in 1929.

Western University - located in Quindaro, Kan., founded in 1865, private, affiliated with the African Methodist Episcopal Church, closed in 1943.

• •

ALABAMA AGRICULTURAL AND MECHANICAL UNIVERSITY

History

Alabama Agricultural and Mechanical University—also known as Alabama A&M University or AAMU—is a public, historically black, land-grant university located in Normal, Madison County, AL, United States. AAMU is a member-school of the Thurgood Marshall College Fund. Fully accredited by the SACS, as well as other specialty, regional and national accrediting bodies. AAMU's academic programs have been recognized by Diverse Issues in Higher Education, Washington Monthly, and US News and World Report. AAMU was originally established by an act of the Alabama State Legislature in 1873 as the State Normal School and University for the Education of the Colored Teachers and Students. In 1919, the school became the State Agricultural and Mechanical Institute for Negroes, and in 1948, it was renamed as the Alabama Agricultural and Mechanical College. In 1939, the State Board of Education granted authority to offer course work on the senior college level.

Relevant Information

Established: 1875

Type: Public, HBCU

Location: 4900 Meridan St. N, Huntsville, AL 35811

Phone: 256-372-5000

Religious Affiliation: NA

Student Enrollment: 5,523

Tuition Fees: In-state $8,586; out-of-state $15,576

Academic Staff: NA

Campus: Suburban, 880 acres

School Colors: Maroon and white

Mascot/Nickname: Bulldogs

Athletics/Sports Affiliation: NCAA Div. I, SWAG, FCS

Endowment: $119 million

Notable Alumni

Louis Crews: former head football coach with winningest record at AAMU.

Don Calloway: member of Missouri House of Representatives.

Dannette Young: winner of Olympic gold and silver medals in track sports.

Marc Lacy: author, lecturer, and government contractor

Shewanda Pugh: author.

Charles Scales: retired deputy administrator for NASA.

Howard Ballard: former NFL player.

Michael Crooms: music producer.

Robert Mathis: NFL defensive end for the Indianapolis Colts

Frank Kearse: NFL defensive tackle for the Carolina Panthers

Jamaal Johnson: NFL defensive lineman.

Fernandez Shaw: Arena Football League defensive end

Sun Ra: jazz musician.

Bama Boyz: music producer.

Mickell Gladness: former NBA player.

Mfana Futhi Bhembe: former soccer player who played in soccer leagues in Swaziland.

Sylvester Croom: minister and community leader in Tuscaloosa, AL

John Stallworth: NFL Hall of Fame member with Pittsburgh Stealers.

Ruben Studdard: participated in American Idol.

Barry Wagner: former Arena Football League player.

Kendrick Rogers: former NFL player.

Vann Pettaway: former men's head basketball coach.

Cleon Jones: former Major League baseball player.

Brick Haley: NFL and college football defensive coach.

Jean Harbor: former soccer play for the Bulldogs who went on to play in various leagues in Nigeria and the United States.

Pearlie M. L. Jenkins: female basketball standout, first Bulldog to dunk in a game.

Lwazi Maziya: former Bulldog soccer player who went on to play with Mbabane Swallows of the Swazi Premier League and the Swaziland national football team.

ALABAMA STATE UNIVERSITY

History

Alabama State University was founded in 1856 as the Lincoln Normal School in Marion, AL. In 1973, the State Board acceptedthe transfer of the school after a legislative act was passed authorizing the state to fund a Normal School. In 1874, this predecessor of Alabama State University became America's first state-supported educational institution for blacks. This began Alabama State University's history as a "Teacher's College." In the years ahead Lincoln Normal became a junior college and in 1928 became a full four-year institution. In 1929, it became State Teachers College for Negroes and in 1948 and in 1954 became Alabama State College. In 1969, the State Board of Education, then the governing body of the university, approved a name change, becoming Alabama State University.

Relevant Information

Established: 1867

Type: Public, HBUC

Location: 915·S Jackson St., Montgomery, AL 36104

Phone: 334-229-4100

Religious Affiliation: NA

Student Enrollment: 12,000

Tuition Fees: In-state $4,508; out-of-state $8,516

Academic Staff: NA

Campus: Urban, 172 acres

School Colors: Black and old gold

Mascot/Nickname: Hornets

Athletics/Sports Affiliation: NCAA Div. I

Endowment: 78 million

Notable Alumni

Joe L. Reed: civil rights pioneer.

W. C. Patton: leader.

Ralph D. Abernathy: civil rights leader and minister.

Fred Gray: attorney.

Fred Shuttlesworth: civil rights leader and cofounder of SCLC.

Fred Wesley: jazz musician and trombonist.

Eugene Sawyer: politician and former mayor of Chicago.

China Jude: first black female athletic director of Cheyney State University.

Yvonne Kennedy: former president of Bishop State Community College.

J. B. Calloway: Broadway actor.

Clarence Carter: American soul singer and musician.

Rickey Smiley: comedian and actor.

Dionne Walters: contestant on American's Next Top Model.

Jesse White: thirty-seventh secretary of state of Illinois.

Doug Williams: comedian and actor.

Brad Baxter: NFL running back.

Eddie Robinson: NFL football player.

Erskine Hawkins: jazz musician.

Felix Stalling: electronic artist and producer.

James Daniel: coach of the Pittsburgh Steelers.

Jessie Tompkins: former track and field coach for Montgomery Track Club.

Kefa Hare: actor, educator, and motivational speaker.

Lewis Jackson: NBA player and educator.

London Charles: winner of a reality show.

Marcus Winn: linebacker for Canadian Football League.

Quinton Ross: member of Alabama senate.

Ralph Simpson: first African American to earn PhD in music from Michigan State University.

Many Martin: former Buffalo Bills football player. Michael Coe: NFL defensive back.

Reggie Barlow: former professional football player and head football coach at Alabama State University.

Steven Daniel: comedian and actor.

Tangi Miller: actress with the WB'S *Felicity*.

Tarvaris Jackson: Buffalo Bills football player.

Tauheed Epps: rapper known as Two Chainz.

Woody McCorvey: football coach for Mississippi State Bulldogs.

ALBANY STATE UNIVERSITY

History

Albany State University is a four-year, state-supported, historically black university (HBCU) located in Albany, GA. It is one of the three HBCUs in the University System of Georgia. It is a member-school of the Thurgood Marshall College Fund.

W. E. DuBois inspired Joseph W. Holley, born in 1874 to former slaves, to continue his education at Phillips Academy in Andover, MA. DuBois persuaded Holley to return to the South to start a school. Holley organized a board of trustees and purchased 50 acres of land for a campus to provide an education for blacks. The school became financially supported by the state in 1917, as a two-year agricultural and teacher training college under the new name of Georgia Normal and Agricultural College. In 1932, the school became a part of the University System of Georgia, and in 1943, it was granted four-year status. In 1981, the college offered its graduate program, and in 1996, the name was changed to Albany State University.

Relevant Information

Established: 1903

Type: Public, HBCU

Location: 504 College Dr., Albany, GA 31705

Phone: 229-430-4746

Religious Affiliation: NA

Student Enrollment: 4,176

Tuition Fees: In-state $4,402; out-of-state $16,016

Campus: Urban, 231 acres

School Colors: Old gold and royal blue

Mascot/Nickname: Rams

Athletics/Sports Affiliations: NCAA Div. II, SIAC

Endowment: $1,540,666

Notable Alumni

James Blaylock: member of Georgia Department of Veterans Service.

Alice Coachman: first African American woman to win an Olympic gold medal.

Walter Curry: former professional football player.

Gregory Daniels: first African American VP of Nissan North America.

Kenneth Gant: former professional football player.

Jonnie Mae Gibson: fifth African American woman in FBI.

Big James Henderson: former powerlifter, winning five world bench press titles.

Art Green: former CFL and NFL player.

James Holmes: first African American director of US Census Bureau.

Caldwell Jones: former professional basketball player.

Charles Jones: former professional basketball player.

Major Jones: former professional basketball player.

Wil Jones: former professional basketball player.

Dan Land: former professional football player.

Jo Marie Payton: actress.

Bernice J. Reagon: singer, composer, scholar, and social activist.

Shirley Sherrod: civil rights advocate and former Georgia state director of Rural Development for the US Department of Agriculture.

Albert Sloan: twelfth president of Miles College.

Phelan Thomas: first African American cosmetic dentist certified as Diplomate of the American Board of Aesthetic Dentistry.

Rick Ross: rapper.

Mike White: former professional football player and head football coach at Albany State University.

ALCORN STATE UNIVERSITY

History

Alcorn State University is a historically black, comprehensive, land-grant institution in Lorman, MS. It was founded in 1871 by the Reconstruction Era legislature to provide higher education for freedman. It was the first black land-grant college in the United States. It was founded on the site originally occupied by Oakland College, a school for whites established by the Presbyterian Church.

Oakland College closed its doors at the beginning of the American Civil War in order that its students could fight for the Confederate States of America. When the college failed to reopen at the end of the war, the property was sold to the state of Mississippi. It renamed the facility as Alcorn University in honor of James Alcorn in 1871 as the state established it as a historically black college. In 1874, Alcorn Agricultural and Mechanical College became Alcorn State University. Alcorn State is now fully accredited with seven school and degree programs.

Relevant Information

Established: 1871

Type: Public, HBCU, first black land-grant college

Location: 1000 ASU Dr., Alcorn, MS 39096

Phone: 601-877-6100

Religious Affiliation: NA

Student Enrollment: 4,395

Tuition Fees: In=state $5,256; out-of-state $12,912

Academic Staff: NA

Campus: Rural, 1,700 acres

School Colors: Purple and gold

Mascot/Nickname: Braves

Athletics/Sports Affiliation: SWAC, NCAA Div. I

Endowment: $8,823,677

Notable Alumni

Jack Spinks: former professional football player for the New York Giants.

Jimmy Giles: former professional football player for the Tampa Bay Buccaneers.

Roynell Young: former professional football player for the Philadelphia Eagles.

Jack Phillips: former professional football player for the Kansas City Chiefs.

Milton Mack: former professional football player for the Detroit Lions

Cedric Tillman: former professional football player for the Denver Broncos.

Dwayne White: former professional football player for the St. Louis Rams.

Garry Lewis: former professional football player for the Oakland Raiders.

Torrence Small: former professional football player for the New Orleans Saints.

John Thierry: former professional football player for the Chicago Bears.

Steve McNair: former professional football player for the Tennessee Titans and Baltimore Ravens.

Bryant mix: former professional football player for the Houston Oilers.

Donte Dowers: former professional football player for the Baltimore Ravens.

Carlos Thorton: former professional football player for the San Francisco 49ers.

Terry Wilkerson: former professional football player for the Arizona Cardinals.

Donald Driver: current professional football player for the Green Bay Packers.

Charles L. Jackson: former professional football player for the New York Jets.

Orlando Kilaease: chair of Mississippi State Farm Service.

Iris Kyle: female professional bodybuilder.

Kimberly Morgan: Miss Mississippi 2007.

Michael C. Duncan: actor.

Alexander O'Neal: musician.

Ed Smith: former alderman in Chicago, IL.

Jesse Smith: appeared as "Justice" in revival of *American Gladiators*.

Joseph E. Walker: president of Universal Life Insurance Co., Memphis, TN.

Timon K. Durrett: actor.

Albert Butler: Mississippi state senator.

Horace R. Cayton: journalist and politician.

Katie G. Dorsett: member of North Carolina senate.

Medgar Evedrs: first NAACP field secretary.

Alex Haley: author of *Roots: The Saga of an American Family*.

Lee T. Moore: former free agent for the Oakland Raiders.

Chad Slaughter: former professional football player for the Oakland Raiders.

Reynard Reynolds: current AFL player.

Kris Peters: current AFL player.

Marco Walder: former AFL player.

Terrence Crimiel: former AFL player.

Louis Green: former AFL player for the Denver Broncos.

Charlie Spiller: former AFL player for the Tampa Bay Buccaneers.

Nate Hughes: currently NFL player for the Detroit Lions.

Leslie Frazier: head coach, defensive coordinator of Minnesota Vikings, and former special coach of the Indianapolis Colts.

Larry Smith: former NBA player and assistant coach in the NBA and WNBA.

Malcolm Jones: first black head coach at McComb High School in Mississippi.

Lee Robinson: professional football player for the Tampa Bay Buccaneers and Denver Broncos.

Emmanuel Arceneaux: currently CFL and NFL player.

Frank Purnell: former professional football player for the Green Bay Packers.

ALLEN UNIVERSITY

History

Allen University is a private, coeducational, historically black university located in Columbia, SC It has over 600 students and still serves as a predominantly black constituency. Allen University was founded in Cokesbury in 1870 as Payne Institute. Its initial mission was to provide education to freed African American slaves. In 1880, it was moved to Columbia and renamed Allen University in honor of Bishop Richard Allen, founder of the AME Church. The university remains connected to the denomination, which is in the Methodist family of churches. Allen University initially focused on training ministers and teachers and over the years has enlarged its scope to produce graduates in other academic areas.

Relevant Information

Established: 1870

Type: Private, HBCU

Location: 1530 Harden St., Columbia, SC 29204

Phone: 803-376-5700

Religious Affiliation: AME Church

Student Enrollment: 600

Tuition Fees: $11,940

Academic Staff: NA

Campus: Urban; size NA

School Colors: Blue and gold

Mascot/Nickname: Yellow Jackets

Athletics/Sports Affiliations: NAJA, EIAC

Endowment: $307,322

Notable Alumni

Sam Davis: former professional American football player.

George Harold: former professional American football player.

Joseph Delaine: minister and civil rights leader with South Carolina NAACP.

Kay Patterson: member of the South Carolina senate.

AMERICAN BAPTIST COLLEGE

History

American Baptist College (also known as American Baptist Theological Seminary or ABTS) is a small, predominantly African American liberal arts college located in Nashville, TN. In 1924, its predecessor, Roger Williams University, a black college, was primarily designed to train African American Baptist ministers. Its student body was highly influential in the civil rights movement. In March 2013, the college was granted the honor of being named a historically black college and university. In 1971, the school became accredited, and its official name was changed to American Baptist College.

Relevant Information

Established: 1924

Type: Private, HBCU

Location: 1800 Baptist World Center Dr., Nashville, TN 37207

Phone: 615-256-1463

Religious Affiliation: National Baptist Convention, USA, Inc.

Enrollment: 103

Tuition Fees: $5,424

Academic Staff: 20

Campus: Urban, 53 acres

School Colors: Maroon and white

Mascot/Nickname: Huskies

Athletics/Sports Affiliation: CAN

Endowment: NA

Notable Alumni

John Lewis: Georgia Congressman.

James Bevel: civil rights leader.

R. E. Cooper: pastor and civil rights leader.

Leroy Gilbert Jr.: senior pastor of the First Cathedral.

Forest E. Harris Sr.: scholar and author.

Cleavant Derricks: pastor, director, and songwriter.

Julius R. Scruggs: pastor, scholar, and president of National Baptist Convention, USA, Inc.

C. T. Vivian: author, minister, and activist.

Riggins R. Earl Jr.: author, scholar, and ethicist.

Bernard Lafayette: civil rights leader.

UNIVERSITY OF ARKANSAS
AT PINE BLUFF

History

The UAPB is a historically black university located in Pine Bluff, AR. Founded in 1873, it is the oldest HBCU and the second oldest public institution in the state of Arkansas. UAPB is known by its moniker the "Flagship of the Delta." It was authorized by the Reconstruction Era legislature as the Branch Normal College. It was part of the "normal" department of Arkansas Industrial University, later the University of Arkansas. It was operated separately as part of a compromise to get a college for blacks as the state maintained racial segregation well into the twentieth century. In 1890, the state maintained segregated systems to establish a separate land-grant university for blacks as well as for whites. In 1927, the school severed its ties with the University of Arkansas and became Arkansas Mechanical and Normal College. Later, the college rejoined what is now the University of Arkansas System. As a full-fledged campus with a graduate study department, it gained its current name and university status in the process.

Relevant Information

Established: 1873

Type: Public, HBCU

Location: 1200 University Dr., Pine Bluff, AR 71601

Phone: 870-575-8000

Religious Affiliation: NA

Student Enrollment: 3,232

Tuition Fees: In-state $16,562; out-of-state $21,962

Academic Staff: NA

Campus: Urban, 318 acres

School Colors: Black and gold

Mascot/Nickname: Golden Lions

Athletics/Sports Affiliation: NCAA Div. I, SAC, FCS

Endowment: $1,656,751

Notable Alumni

Samuel L. Kountz: performed first successful kidney transplant between humans who were not identical twins.

Terron Armstead: NFL offensive lineman with the New Orleans Saints.

Benjamin L. Pruitt: music educator.

Martha S. Lewis: government official in the New York City and state.

Danny K. Davis: US Representative in Illinois.

Jamil Nasser: jazz musician and bassist.

Frank Burgess: professional basketball player and an attorney.

Joe Gardner: jazz musician and trumpet.

Cleophus Charles: Carter Woodson Professorship recipient.

David D. Chapple: musician, saxophonist, and bandleader.

John Stubblefield: jazz musician, saxophonist, and recording artist.

James Leary: jazz classical musician and bass player.

L. C. Greenwood: former football player with Pittsburgh Steelers.

Cleo Miller: former football player.

Ivory L Brown: former football player.

Smokie Norful: pastor, gospel singer, and pianist.

Jamil Snowden: football player.

Chris Akins: former NFL football player.

Big Tuck: rapper.

Greg· Wesley: NFL football player.

Dante Wesley: football player.

Courtney V. Buren: former NFL football player.

Charles Ali: former football player with the Cleveland Browns.

Martell Mallett: football player.

Don Zimmerman: former football player.

ARKANSAS BAPTIST COLLEGE

History

Arkansas Baptist College is a private, historically black, liberal arts college located in Little Rock, AR. Founded in 1884 as a Minister's Institute. ABC was initially funded by the Colored Baptists of the State of Arkansas. It is the only HBCU west of the Mississippi River. It committed to nurturing those of African American heritage but open and available to students of all backgrounds. In addition to areas like religious studies, ABC also offers academics in business, arts, and humanities and social studies. Regarding the spiritual and the intellectual as equally important, ABC's religious activities are an integral part of campus life. Chapel services and religious lectures from guest are held regularly on campus for students and faculty.

Relevant Information

Established: 1884

Type: Private, HBCU

Location: 1621 Martin Luther King Dr., Little Rock, AR 72206

Phone: 501-370-4000

Religious Affiliation: Baptist

Student Enrollment: 626

Tuition Fees: In-state $6,960; out-of-state

$18,722

Academic Staff: NA

Campus: Urban; acre size, NA

School Colors: Purple and white

Mascot/Nickname: Buffalos

Athletics/Sports Affiliation: NCAA, Div. II, SIAC

Endowment: $97,497

Notable Alumni

Emerald Crosby: president of North Central Association of College Accreditation.

Glenda Black: founder, editor, and publisher of *Good News* magazine.

Rev. Joseph C. Crenchaw: civil rights activist.

BARBER-SCOTIA COLLEGE

History

Barber-Scotia College is a historically black college located in Concord, NC. It began as a female seminary in 1867. Scotia Seminary was chartered in 1870 through the Presbyterian Church to prepare young African American southern women for careers as social workers and teachers. It was one of the first black institutions built after the Civil War for giving black women an alternate to becoming servants of field hands. Scotia Seminary was modeled after Mount Holyoke Female Seminary (now Mount Holyoke College) and was referred to as the Mount Holyoke of the South. It is listed in the National Register of Historic Places and is one of the only four nineteenth century institutional buildings left in Cabarrus County. After closing during the 1970s due to lack of funds for its maintenance, it was renamed to Scotia Women's College in 1916. In 1930, the seminary was merged with another female institution, Barber Memorial College, and became Barber-Scotia College. After losing its accreditation and establishing partnerships with other accredited institutions, Barber-Scotia struggled to stay afloat.

Relevant Information

Established: 1867

Type: Private, HBCU

Location: 145 Cabarrus Ave. West, Concord, NC 28025

Phone: 704-789-2900

Religious Affiliation: Presbyterian Church Student

Enrollment: 120

Tuition Fees: In-state and out-of- state

$9,300 Academic Staff: NA

Campus: Urban, 23 acres

Schools Colors: Royal blue and Gray

Mascot/Nickname: Tiger

Athletics/Sports Affiliation: NAIA, EIAC

Endowment: NA

Notable Alumni

Mary McLeod Bethune: adviser to President Franklin D. Roosevelt and past president of Bethune-Cookman College.

Katie G. Cannon: the first African American female ordained minister by the Presbyterian Church.

Ida V. Smith: an early aviatrix.

BENEDICT COLLEGE

History

Benedict College is a historically black, liberal arts college located in Columbia, SC. Founded in 1870 by northern Baptists, it was originally a teachers college. Benedict was founded on a 110-acre plantation in Columbia, SC. The Baptist Home Mission Society provided $13,000 to purchase the land to open Benedict Institute in 1870 for the recently emancipated people of African descent. In 1894, the institution was chartered as a liberal arts college by the South Carolina Legislature and named Benedict College. In 1994, with strategic planning process in place, the college set an enrollment goal of "2,000" by the end of the year 2000. The goal was achieved in 1996 with an enrollment of 2,138 students. The fall of 2002, enrollment was at 3,000. The college is currently implementing a $50 million campus improvement plan, which includes land acquisition and the completion of a comprehensive athletics complex.

Relevant Information

Established: 1870

Type: Private, HBCU

Location: 1600 Harden St., Columbia, SC 29204

Phone: 803-253-5000

Religious Affiliation: American Baptist Churches, USA

Student Enrollment: 2,500

Tuition Fees: $17,190

Academic Staff: NA

Campus: Urban, 110 acres

School Colors: Purple and gold

Mascot/Nickname: Tigers

Athletics/Sports Affiliation: NCAA Div. II, SIAC

Endowment: NA

Notable Alumni

Modjeska M. Simkins: leader of African American public health reform and civil rights movement in South Carolina.

Harold A. Stevens: lawyer and former judge who served on the New Court of General Sessions and Appeals.

Jack B. Johnson: former county executive for Prince George's County, MD.

LeRoy T. Walker: former US Olympic Committee chairman. Howie Bell: comedian.

Waliyy Dixon: professional streetball player.

Kris Bruton: basketball player who currently plays with the Harlem Globetrotters.

BENNETT COLLEGE

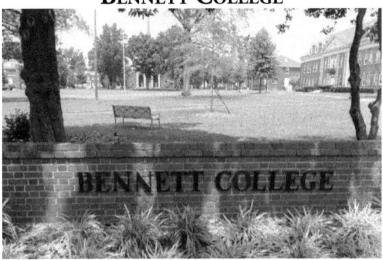

History

B ennett College is a four-year, liberal arts women's college in Greensboro, NC. Founded in 1873, this historically black institution began as a normal school to provide education to newly emancipated slaves. It became a women's college in 1926 and, today, it serves 780 undergraduates. Bennett College is one of the only two historically black colleges for women in the United States. It has struggled for years with financial difficulties and was briefly placed on probation by its regional accrediting body in 2011 for operating a foul of the accreditor's standard on financial stability. In 1916, after doing research and finding there was no collegiate-level institution for African American women, Bennett was chartered as a college for women by the Home Missionary Society and the Board of Education made Bennett a college for women. After ten years of searching for a location, Bennett was fully transitioned into a Women's college in 1926. Dr. Willa B. Player was named the first African American woman to be president of the college.

Relevant Information

Established: 1873

Type: Private, Women's HBCU

Location: 900 E Washington St., Greensboro, NC 27401 Phone: 336-137 8677

Religious Affiliation: Methodist Student Enrollment: 780

Tuition Fees: $16,794

Academic Staff: NA

Campus: Urban, 55 acres

School Colors: Blue and white

Mascot/Nickname: Belles

Athletics/Sports affiliation: USCAA and NCAA Div. III

Endowment: $15 million

Notable Alumni

Dorothy L. Brown: first African American woman as general surgeon in the South to serve on the Tennessee State Legislature.

Maidie Norman: actress and educator.

Sandra N. Smith: activist and Bennett College student government association president killed by the KKK as she protested unfair wages.

Lady Sara Lou Harris: first African American model to appear in national advertisements.

Carolyn A. Payton: first African American woman and first psychologist tapped by President Jimmy Carter to head the Peace Corps.

Frances J. Bonner: first African American physician to become a faculty member at Massachusetts General Hospital in Boston.

Allethia L. Allen: professor emeritus of University of Washington.

Fay Robinson: opera singer, soprano, currently an artist in residence at University of Arizona.

Linda B. Brown: author, educator, civil rights activist and distinguished professor in humanities at Bennett.

Kimberly M. Cuthrell: author of *My Soul.*

Michelle Huff: founder of Huff Entertainment.

Hattie Caldwell: research scientist and expert in radiation. Gladys Robinson: serving senator of Greensboro, NC.

Glendora M. Putnam: civil rights attorney and former president of National YWCA.

Roslyn Smith: civil rights activist and one in the Greensboro sit-ins. Amikka Smith: news anchor/reporter.

Tammi McCall: actress, radio host, TV host of the show *Gossip Queens.*

Andrea Harris: president and cofounder of the North Carolina Institute of Minority Economic Development.

Rev. Sekinah Hamlin: former director of Multicultural Education at Guilford College.

Belinda Foster: first African American district attorney in North Carolina.

Talia McCray: noted research scientist.

Barbara L. Hamm: fourth African American female television news director in the United States.

Yvonne J. Johnson: first African American mayor of Greensboro, NC.

Patrida L. Brown: former moderator of Presbyterian Church.

Marion L. Bell: noted educator.

Marissa Jennings: founder and CEO of Socialgrlz LLC.

Mary Jacobs: former Durham city council at Large.

Patrice Vailes-Macarie: former runway model and currently a fashion advisor for Lord & Taylor.

Joyce M. Dixon: cofounder of Creative Management Technology.

Jacquelyn Grant: author of widely acclaimed *White Women's Christ and Black Women's Jesus.*

Beverly Buchanan: noted artist for her exploration of Southern Vernacular Architecture.

Chaundra Luckett: producer at WAGA-TV. Fox 5 in Atlanta.

Alexis Mitchell: Emmy Award-winning journalist.

Joyce Garrett: founder and advisor of the Washington Youth Choir.

Myrtle L Brown: professor, noted nutritionist, and government research scientist.

Lillie M. Jones: pastor & nationally distinguished educator & sought after speaker.

Shauntae Smith: youth pastor at Crown Ministries International.

Hideko T. Snider: a Hiroshima, Japan, nuclear bomb survivor and author of *One Sunny Day.*

Valerie Callendar: internationally recognized dermatologist.

BETHUNE-COOKMAN UNIVERSITY

History

Bethune-Cookman University, or B-CU, is a private, historically black university in Daytona Beach, Fl. Mary McLeod Bethune founded the Daytona Educational and Industrial Training School in 1904. The school underwent several stages of growth and development through the years, and in 1923, it merged with the Cookman Institute of Jacksonville, FL, and became a coed high school. In 1924, it became affiliated with the Methodist Church.

By 1931, the school became a junior college. The name was changed in 1941 to Bethune College when the Florida Board of Education approved a four-year baccalaureate program. In February 14, 2007, the board of trustees approved the name Bethune-Cookman University. Bethune-Cookman meets its commitment to excellence through expanding and modifying academic programs and innovative curricular offerings by preparing students to meet the demands of the future.

Relevant Information

Established: 1904

Type: Private, HBCU

Location: 640 Dr. Mary Mcleod Bethune Blvd., Daytona Beach, FL

31

32114

Phone: 386-481-2000

Religious Affiliation: Unite Methodist Church

Student Enrollment: 3,594

Tuition Fees: $28,608

Academic Staff: NA

Campus: Urban, 82 acres

School Colors: Maroon and gold

Mascot/Nickname: Wildcats

Athletics/Sports Affiliation: NCAA, MEAC Div. I

Endowment: $34 million

Notable Alumni

Marjorie Joyner: inventor of permanent wave machine.

Lucille O'Neal: mother of NBA player Shaquille O'Neal.

Evelyn Bethune: CEO of Mary Bethune Education Legacy Foundation.

Harry T. Moore: civil rights leader.

Henry Lyons: former president of National Baptist Convention, USA, Inc.

Yvonne S. Golden: educator, activist, first black mayor of Daytona Beach, FL.

Rodney Chester: actor.

Marc "DJ Naiz" Dixon: radio personality.

Kevin J. Woods: actor.

James Bush: member of Florida House of Representatives.

William H. Turner: first African American chair of Miami-Dade County School Board.

Larry Little: former NFL player and member of Pro Football Hall of Fame.

John Chaney: former head basketball coach at Temple University.

Cy McClairen: first Bethume-Cookman alumnus in NFL.

Alvin Wyatt: former NFL player and head football coach at Bethune-Cookman.

Rashean Mathis: NFL cornerback.

Eric Weens: NFL wide receiver.

Nick Collins: NFL player.

Terry Anderson: NFL player.

Stevie Baggs: NFL and Canadian football player.

Ruby Barber: former AFL Player.

Sebastian Boucher: Minor League prospect.

Rickey Claitt: former NFL player.

Booble Clark: former NFL player.

Damian Cook: former NFL player.

Kevin F. Aka Kimbo Slice: martial arts and street fighter.

Stan Jefferson: former Major League baseball player.

Maulty Moore: former NFL Player.

Aulcie Perry: former professional basketball player.

Clifford Reed: former men's head basketball coach at Bethune-Cookman.

Booker Reed: former NFL player.

Charles Riggine: former NFL player.

Jerry Simmons: former NFL player.

T. T. Toliver: Arena Football League player.

Lee Williams: former NFL player.

Mark Woodyard: Major League baseball player.

Antron Wright: former NFL player.

BISHOP STATE COMMUNITY COLLEGE

History

Bishop State Community College is a state-supported, two-year, public, historically black college (HBCU) founded in 1927. In 1965, a legislative act officially declared "Alabama State College Branch Mobile Center" a state junior college. In 1965, the college was named "Mobile State Junior College." The name was changed in 1971 to "S. D. Bishop State Junior College" and again in 1989 to "Bishop State Community College." In 1991, the Alabama State Board of Education consolidated Southwest State Technical College and Carver State Technical College into Bishop State Community College. The college is located in Mobile, AL.

Relevant Information

Established: 1927

Type: Public, HBCU

Location: 351 N Broad St., Mobile, AL 36603

Phone: 252-405-7000

Religious Affiliation: NA

Student Enrollment: 3,982

Tuition Fees: In-state and out-of-state $10,463 Academic Staff: NA

Campus: Four campuses; size, NA

School Colors: Green and gold

Mascot/Nickname: Wildcats

Athletics/Sports Affiliation: ACCA and NJCAA

Endowment: $27 million

Notable Alumnus

Jessie Tompkins: former national-rank athlete in track and field.

BLUEFIELD STATE COLLEGE

History

Bluefield State College is a historically black college located in Bluefield, WV. The school is not in any way connected with Bluefield College in nearby Bluefield, VA. According to its charter, the institution was founded in 1895 as Bluefield Colored Institute and created a high school for the Negro youth in the nearby area. In the late 1920s, the students and staff of the school referred to it as Bluefield Institute, but the name was never sanctioned by the West Virginia Legislature. By September 1954, state-supported colleges in West Virginia were integrated. Three white students in a total body of 354 enrolled at Bluefield State. During the late 1960s, black students protested that the state was transforming the school from a traditional black college to a white commuter college. In 1968, racial tensions culminated in the bombing of the gymnasium. After the bombing of the school's gym, which resulted in closing of the school's dormitories that housed a significant number of the college's black students, this hastened the transition to a predominant white college. The racial ratio is now 81.95 percent white as opposed to 12.77 percent black.

Relevant Information

Established: 1895

Type: Public, HBCU

Location: 219 Rock St., Bluefield, WV 24701

Phone: 304-327-4000

Religious Affiliation: NA

Student Enrollment: 2,063

Tuition Fees: In-state $5,180; out-of-state $9,944

Academic Staff: 145

Campus: Rural, 50 acres

School Colors: Royal blue and gold

Mascot/nickname: Big Blue

Athletics/Sports Affiliation: NCAA Div. II

Endowment: $1,364,035

Notable Alumni

Maceo Pinkard: musician and songwriter.

William Gray: former president of Florida A&M University.

Elizabeth Drewry: first African American female elected to West Virginia Legislature.

Cecil B. Moore: Philadelphia lawyer and City councilman. Dan C. Bowling: member of the Virginia House of Delegates.

Rick Snuffer: member of the Virginia House of Delegates.

Thomas W. Anderson: minister and NAACP president.

BOWIE STATE UNIVERSITY

History

Bowie State University (Bowie State) is a public university located on 338 acres in unincorporated Prince George's County, MD, north of the suburban city of Bowie. Bowie State is part of the University System of Maryland. It is Maryland's oldest historically black university and one of the ten oldest in the country. It is a member-school of the Thurgood Marshall College Fund. In partnership with the University of Maryland University College, Bowie State University became the first historically black to include overseas studies. It was also the first university in the nation to offer a bachelor's degree in pedology. In 1995, NASA and the National Science Foundation awarded $27 million as one of the only six schools in the nation declared Model Institutions for Excellence in science, engineering, and mathematics. This led to the strengthening of the already growing computer science program. The university is home to the Maryland Center, a not-for-profit organization founded in 1998.

Relevant Information

Established: 1865

Type: Public, HBCU

Location: 14000 Jericho Park Rd., Bowie, MD 20715

Phone: 301-860-4000

Religious Affiliation: NA

Student Enrollment: 5,600

Tuition Fees: In-state $19,897; out-of-state $30,453 Academic Staff: 400

Campus: Suburban, 338 acres

School Colors: Black and gold

Mascot/Nickname: Bulldogs

Athletics/Sports Affiliation: NCAA Div. II, CIM

Endowment: $23,991,522

Notable Alumni

David Lindsey: songwriter, producer, and member of the singing group 7 Sons of Soul.

Dante Lee: marketing guru and president and CEO of Dante Lee and cofounder of Lee Moss Media.

Joanne Benson: Maryland state delegate.

Gwendolyn T. Britt: Maryland state senator.

Toni Braxton: singer and songwriter.

Towanda Braxton: singer, songwriter, and member of the singing group The Braxtons.

Isaac Redman: NFL running back for the Pittsburgh Steelers.

Wale Folarin: DC rapper.

Henry Frazier Ill: head football coach at Bowie State University, PVAMU, and NCCU.

Christa McAuliffe: teacher-astronaut killed in space shuttle accident.

James L. Walls: mayor, City of District Heights, MD, and president of World Conference of Mayors.

CENTRAL STATE UNIVERSITY

History

Central State University—commonly referred to as CSU—is a historically black university (HBCU) located in Wilberforce, OH. It is the only HBCU in Ohio. It is a member-school of the Thurgood Marshall College Fund. CSU's history began when Wilberforce College was privately established in Tawawa Springs, OH, in 1856. This was founded as a merger between the Cincinnati Conference of the Methodist Episcopal Church and the AME Church. In 1887, the Ohio General Assembly enacted legislation to create the Combined Normal and Industrial Department at Wilberforce College to provide training for teachers of lower grades and vocational education. This department operated as a part of Wilberforce University. In 1941, the Combined Normal and Industrial Department expanded from a two-year to a four-year program. It was legally split from Wilberforce College in 1947 when it became the College of Education and Industrial Arts at Wilberforce, OH. In 1951, it was renamed as Central State College, and in 1965, the institution achieved university status.

Relevant Information

Established: 1887

Type: Public, HBCU

Location: 1400 Brush Row Rd., Wilberforce, OH 45384

Phone: 937-376-6011

Religious Affiliation: Methodist Episcopal Church

Student Enrollment: 2,798

Tuition Fees: In-state $5,292; out-of-state $11,462

Academic Staff: NA

Campus: Rural, 638 acres

School Colors: Maroon and gold
Mascot/Nickname: Marauders

Athletics/Sports Affiliation: NCAA Div. II, GMAC Endowment: $2,146,429

Notable Alumni

Hastings K. Banda: former president of Malawi.

Vince Buck: former NFL defensive back for the New Orleans Saints.

Wayne A. Cauthen: first African American appointed as city manager of Kansas City, MO.

Clay Dixon: former city commissioner and mayor of Dayton, OH.

Hugh Douglas: former NFL lineman for the New York Jets and

Philadelphia Eagles.

Arsenio Hall: honorary doctor of humane letters degree.

Vince Heflin: former NFL wide receiver for the Miami Dolphins and Tampa Buccaneers.

James T. Henry: first black mayor and city council of Xenia, OH.

Charles Hope: former Green Bay Packers guard and NFL player. Priest Lauderdale: former NBA player for the Denver Nuggets.

Omarosa M. Stallworth: actress.

Kedar Massenberg: record label producer.

Eddie Miner: professional baseball player for the Cincinnati Reds and San Francisco Giants.

Rob Murphy: assistant basketball coach at Syracuse University.

Leontyne Price: opera singer.

John Roseboro: former professional baseball player.

John W. Shamon: US undersecretary of the army.

Teddy Seymour: first African American to sail around the world solo.

Jason Thomas: 9/11 hero and keynote speaker.

Kerwin Waldroup: former NFL defensive end.

Erik Williams: former Pro Bowl lineman for the Dallas Cowboys and Baltimore Ravens.

Nancy Wilson: jazz singer.

CHEYNEY UNIVERSITY OF PENNSYLVANIA

History

Cheyney University of Pennsylvania is a part of the Pennsylvania State System of Higher Education. It has a 275-acre campus that is located in the Cheyney community within Thornbury Township, Chester County, and Deleware County in the state of Pennsylvania. Cheyney University is a member-school of the Thurgood Marshall College Fund. Founded as the African Institute in 1837 and renamed the Institute of Colored Youth, the institution is the oldest African American institution of higher learning. The school was soon renamed the Institute for Colored Youth, providing training in trades and agriculture as those were the predominant skills needed in the general economy. In 1902, the institute moved to George Cheyney's farm, 25 miles west of Philadelphia. The school's official name changed several times during the twentieth century, Cheyney joined the State System of Higher Education as Cheyney University of Pennnsylvania.

Relevant Information

Established: 1837

Type: Public, HBCU

Location: 1837 University Circle, PO Box 200, Cheyney, PA 19319

Phone: 800-243-9639

Religious Affiliation: NA

Student Enrollment: 1,519

Tuition Fees: In-state $21,458; out-of-state $25,638

Academic Staff: NA

Campus: Suburban, 275 acres

School Colors: Blue and white

Mascot/Nickname: Wolves

Athletics/Sports Affiliation: NCAA, PSAC

Endowment: NA

Notable Alumni

Octavius Gatto: activist and founder of the first black baseball team in the United States.

Martha A. Fairbeau: first female graduate.

Joseph E. Lee: member of Florida House and Senate.

Rebecca J. Cole: second African American woman and first black woman to graduate from Women's Medical College of Pennsylvania.

James B. Dudley: graduated from Institute for Colored Youth around 1875 (now Cheyney).

Robert L. Woodson: neoconservative economic activist with ties to the administrations of Ronald Reagan and George W. Bush.

Gladys S. Johnson: chancellor of the University of Nebraska at Kearney.

Ed Bradley: former CBS News journalist on "60 Minutes."

Jim Vance: Emmy Award-winning anchorman.

William "Billy" Joe: coached and won *237* football games at Cheyney, Central State, and Florida A&M.

Craig Welbourn: owner and operates twenty-eight McDonalds restaurants.

Jim Ellis: inspiration behind movie starring Terrence Howard and Bernie Mac.

Robert Bogle: president/CEO of *Philadelphia Tribune,* the oldest black newspaper in circulation today.

Ronald S. Coleman: lieutenant general and second three-star general of African American heritage in the USMC.

Michael Horsey: former Democratic State Representative.

Samuel J. Patterson: CEO of Shepard-Patterson and Information

Consulting Firm.

Levy L. Simon: award-winning playwright.

Andre Waters: former NFL player.

Dave Warren: talk show radio host; worked at stations WCAU, WDAS, and WHAT, Philadelphia.

Randy Monroe: current head coach of University of Maryland, Baltimore County men's basketball team.

Thaddeus Kirkland: state representative in Delaware County.

James "Big Cat" Williams: former Chicago Bears offensive tackle.

Robert Traynham: openly gay political analyst and television personality on the Comcast Network.

Dominique Curry: NFL player with St. Louis Rams.

Josephine S. Yates: writer, teacher, and civil rights advocate.

Julian Abele: prominent African American architect who designed and contributed to the design of some 250 buildings.

Bayard Rustin: openly gay African American civil rights activist.

S. H. Woodson: first African American to serve as speaker of the New Jersey General Assembly since Reconstruction Era.

Marcus Foster: African American educator who gained national reputation as principal of Gratz High School in Philadelphia.

Joseph M. Segars: US Ambassador to South Africa.

CLAFLIN UNIVERSITY

History

Claflin University is located in Orangeburg, SC. It was founded in 1869 and is the oldest historically black college in the state of South Carolina. Claflin was founded after the American Civil War by Methodist missionaries from Massachusetts to provide education to freedmen and prepare them to take their places as full American citizens. The university was named after two Methodist churchmen, Massachusetts's Governor William Claflin and his brother, philanthropist, Lee Claflin, who provided a large part of the funds to purchase the campus. Claflin secured its charter in 1869 with the forbidding of discrimination of any sort among faculty, staff, and students, making Claflin the first South Carolina university open to all students regardless of race, class, or gender. In 1870, the Baker Biblical Institute merged with Claflin University. The South Carolina General Assembly designated the South State Agricultural and Mechanical Institute as a part of Claflin University.

Relevant Information

Established: 1869

Type: Private, HBCU

Location: 400 Magnolia St., Orangeburg, SC 29115

Phone: 803-535-5000

Religious Affiliation: United Methodist Church

Student Enrollment: 1,920

Tuition/Fees: In-state $6,685; out-of-state $10,600

Academic Staff: NA

Campus: Urban, 40 acres

School Colors: Maroon and orange

Mascot/Nickname: Panther

Athletics/Sports Affiliation: NCAA Div. II, SIAC

Endowment: $20 million

Notable Alumni

Roger K. Williams: educator who taught psychology at four universities.

Danny: recording artist for Okay player Records and music producer/composer for MTVs Hype Music library.

Gloria A. Blackwell: civil rights activist and professor at Clark Atlanta University.

Nathaniel Frederick: professor of communication at Claflin University.

Joseph H. Jefferson: member of South Carolina House of Representatives.

Leonard Pressley: professor of biology at Claflin University.

Leo Twiggs: artist and educator.

CLARK ATLANTA UNIVERSITY

History

Clark Atlanta University is a private, historically black university in Atlanta, GA. It was formed in 1988 by merging Clark College (founded in 1869) and Atlanta University (founded in 1865). Clark Atlanta University is a member of the UNCF. It was founded in 1865 by the AMA. At the same time, Atlanta University affiliated with Morehouse College and Spelman College in a university plan known as the Atlanta University Center. Clark College was founded in 1869. Today, the university offers forty areas of study, including graduate programs in business and education to a racially diverse student body.

Relevant Information

Established: 1988

Type: Private, HBCU

Location: 223 James P. Brawley Dr., Southwest, Atlanta, GA 30314

Phone: 404-880-8000

Religious Affiliation: United Methodist Church

Student Enrollment: 4,000

Tuition Fees: $18,912

Academic Staff: NA

Campus: Urban, 126 acres

School Colors: Red, black, and gray

Mascot/Nickname: Panther

Athletics/Sports Affiliations: NCAA Div. II, SIAC Endowment: $44.2 million

Notable Alumni

Ralph Abernathy: civil rights activist.

Marvin S. Arrington: politician and jurist. Bryan Barber: director of film *Idlewild.*

Benjamin Brown: civil rights activist and member of Georgia State House of Representatives.

Sir Edward Miles: philanthropist.

Aki Collins: assistant men's basketball coach with the Marquette.

Marva Collins: educator and founder of Westside Preparatory School in Chicago.

Mary F. Early: first African American graduate from University of Georgia.

Wayman Carter: composer and first person to use flute excessively in jazz.

Amanda Davis: news anchor at station WAGA in Atlanta, GA.

Pearl Cleage: author.

D. J. Drama: music producer.

Henry 0. Ripper: first African American graduate of West Point.

C. H. Grattan: economist and historian.

Grace T. Hamilton: first African American elected to Georgia General Assembly.

James A. Hefner: economist.

Fletcher Henderson: pianist, bandleader, and composer.

James Weldon Johnson: writer.

New Jack: professional wrestler.

Alexander Jefferson: retired US Air Force lieutenant colonel and Tuskegee Airman.

Robert R. Jennings: president of Alabama Agricultural and Mechanical University.

Henry Johnson: US Congressman from Georgia.

Otis Johnson: mayor of Savannah, GA.

C. L. Grant: TV editor and producer and founder of HBCU unit network.

Reatha C. King: scientist, philanthropist, and educator.

Kenny Leon: actor.

Lucy C. Laney: educator; opened first school for black children in Atlanta, GA.

Curtis Johnson: NFL linebacker.

Walt Landers: NFL player.

Greg McCrary: former NFL light end.

Emmanuel Lewis: actor.

Martha Lewis: government official in New York City and State.

Evelyn G. Lowery: civil rights activist and leader.

Mason D. Betha: rapper.

Harry Pace: African American pioneer and founder of Black Swan Records.

Eva Pigford: model and actress.

Nnegest Likke: movie director and screenwriter.

Jacque Reid: journalist.

Pemessa C. Seele: immunologist.

C. Lamont Smith: sports agent and founder of All Pro Sports and Entertainment.

Moms Stroug: former professional football player.

Horace Tate: Georgia state senator and educator.

Michelle Y. Madison: music executor.

Bobby Wilson: singer.

Phuthuma Nhleko: CEO of MTN Group.

Jo A. Robinson: civil rights activist.

Horace T. Ward: judge.

Lisa Washington: news anchor of WHNT TV, Huntville, AL.

Walter F. While: NAACP.

Hosea Williams: civil rights activist.

Madaline A. Williams: first black woman elected to the New Jersey State Legislature.

Lotis T. Wright: first black surgeon to head the Department of Surgery at Harlem Hospital in New York.

Richard R. Wright: first black paymaster in the US Army and first president of Savannah State University.

Dorothy Yancey: former president of JCSU.

Bla G. Vales: first African American director of Atlanta Fulton Public Library System.

Chaka Zula: hip-hop producer and manager

CLINTON JUNIOR COLLEGE

History

C linton Junior College is a historically black, private, two-year, junior college in Rock Hill, SC. It was founded as the Clinton Institute in 1894 and named after Bishop Galeb L. Clinton, the AME Zion Church's Palmetto Conference presiding bishop at the time. In June 1909, it was incorporated as Clinton Normal and Industrial Institute. It is accredited by the Transnational Association of Christian and Schools. The doors of the institution are opened to all, those who have achieved academically and to those who have yet to reach their full potential. The college continues to provide a learning milieu for students to promote academic achievement and positive moral and spiritual development. This environment fosters leadership qualities and encourages students to be good citizens who can contribute to a global society.

Relevant Information

Established: 1894

Type: Private, HBCU

Location: 1029 Crawford Ret, Rock Hill, SC 29730

Phone: 803-327-7402

Religious Affiliation: AME Zion Church

Student Enrollment: 43

Tuition Fees: $10,035

Academic Staff: NA

Campus: Urban, 100 acres

School Colors: Gold

Mascot/Nickname: Golden Bears

Athletics/Sports Affiliation: NJCAA Div. I

Endowment: $13 million

Notable Alumni

Matt Christopher: children author.

Spanky Anderson: baseball manager.

Jim Hoagland: journalist and Pulitzer Prize winner.

Ironing B. Ham: blues keyboardist.

William I. Long: Tony Award-winning costume designer.

Vernon Grant: commercial artist.

Edmund Lewandowski: precisionist artist.

David Ball: country music singer.

Leon Rippy: actor.

Lauren Cholewinski: Olympic speed skater.

Lafayette Currence: baseball player.

Emery: rock band.

Jim Ray: Major League baseball pitcher.

Jeff Clayton: lead singer of rock band Antiseen.

Jadevon Clowney: defensive end for University of South Carolina

Gamecocks.

Cordarrelle Patterson: former University of Tennessee Volunteers' wide receiver.

Gerald Dixon: former NFL player.

Chris Hope: former NFL player.

Ko Simpson: NFL player.

Benjamin Watson: NFL player.

Rick Sanford: former NFL player.

Phillip Adams: former NFL player.

Donnie Shell: former NFL player.

COAHOMA COMMUNITY COLLEGE

History

Coahoma Community College is a community college and HBCU located in Coahoma County in the state of Mississippi, approximately 4 miles north of the City of Clarksdale. The 99-acre campus lies on an agrarian setting along Clarksdale-Friars Point Road near the Mississippi River. Establishing Coahoma County Agricultural High School in 1924, Coahoma County became the first county in Mississippi to provide an agricultural high school to Negroes under the then existing "separate but equal" doctrine for education. The junior college curriculum was added, and the name of the institution was changed to Coahoma Junior College and Agricultural High School. In 1965, the college opened its doors to all students regardless of race, color, sex, national origin, or disability-With the approval of the of Trustees of Coahoma Junior College and the State Board for Community and Junior Colleges, Coahoma Community College's name was changed to Coahoma Community College, effective from 1989.

Relevant Information

Established: 1924

Type: Public, HBCU

Location: 3240 Friars Point Rd., Clarksdale, MS 38614

Phone: 662-627-2571

Religious Affiliation: NA

Student Enrollment: 2,263

Tuition Fees: In-state and out-of-state $6,554 Academic Staff: NA

Campus: Rural, 99 acres

School Colors: Maroon and white

Mascot/Nickname: Tigers

Athletics/Sports Affiliation: NJCAA

Endowment: NA

Notable Alumni

Jonathan Aldridge: pro athlete and celebrity entertainer.

Tom Johnson: pro athlete with New Orleans Saints.

Dantrell Savage: American League football player.

Brittney Reese: Olympian long jumper.

Terrence Cody: AFL football player.

Eltoro Freeman: AFL football player.

Demond Washington: AFL football player.

Chris White: AFL football player.

CONCORDIA COLLEGE

History

Concordia College in Alabama is a college of the Lutheran Church, located in Salma, AL. It is the only black college among ten colleges in the Concordia System. It is a private, four-year college with a student body of about 700 and with a student-faculty ratio of 21 to 1. Concordia offers degrees across its academic divisions of general education, teacher education, psychology, and business and computers. Outside of the classroom, students participate in a range of student groups such as the Drama Club, the College Choir, and the Millionaires Business Club. The school encourages students to participate in chapel worship, Bible study, and various athletic teams.

Relevant Information

Established: 1922

Type: Private, HBCU

Location: 1712 Broad St., Selma, AL 36701

Phone: 334-874-5700

Religious Affiliation: Lutheran Church

Student Enrollment: 719

Tuition Fees: In-state and out-of-state $8,190 Academic Staff: NA

Campus: Urban, 60 acres

School Colors: Green and yellow

Mascot/Nickname: Hornets

Athletics/Sports Affiliation: NA

Endowment: $4,155,743

Notable Alumni

NA

COPPIN STATE UNIVERSITY

History

Coppin State University was founded in 1900 at what was then called Colored High School and later named Douglas High School that initiated a one-year training course for the preparation of African American elementary teachers. In 1926, the facility was named Fanny Jackson Coppin Normal School in honor of an African American woman who was a pioneer in teacher education, Fanny Jackson Coppin. In 1938, the curriculum of the normal school was lengthened to four years, authority was given for granting of the Bachelor of Science degree, and the name was changed to Coppin Teachers College. In 1950, Coppin became part of the higher education system of Maryland under the State Department of Education and renamed Coppin State Teachers College. In 1988, the college became part of the newly organized University of Maryland System. The school was officially renamed as Coppin State University.

Relevant Information

Established: 1900

Type: Public, HBCU

Location: 2500 W. North Ave., Baltimore, MD 21216

Phone: 410-951-3000

Religious Affiliation: NA

Student Enrollment: 4,000

Tuition Fees: $11,186

Academic Staff: NA

Campus: Urban, 52 acres

School Colors: Blue and gold

Mascot/Nickname: Eagles

Athletics/Sports Affiliation: NCAA Div. I, MEAC, FCS

Endowment: NA

Notable Alumni

Damon Elliott: music and film producer.

Bishop L. Robinson: first African American police commissioner of Baltimore City.

Stephanie Ready: first female coach in professional men's basketball.

Larry Stewart: former NBA player for Washington Bullets and Seattle Super Sonics.

Raheem DeVaughn: R&B Neo-Soul artist.

Tywain McKee: professional basketball player in Australia.

Margaret Murphy: first black woman chair of Baltimore City Delegation.

Cyrus: R&B Neo-Soul artist.

Rafi Reavis: Philippine Basketball Association player.

Dorian Pena: Philippine Basketball Association player.

Verda Welcome: Maryland politician and educator.

Mike Malachi: underground hip-hop artist from Baltimore.

DELAWARE STATE UNIVERSITY

History

Delaware State University (also referred to as DSU, DESU, or Del State) is a historically black, public university located in Dover, DE. DSU has two separate campuses located in Wilmington, DE, and Georgetown, DE. It was established in 1891 by the Delaware General Assembly. The institution became Delaware State College by legislative action. The current population includes a 76 percent African American enrollment and an increasing number of Caucasians, Hispanics, Asians, and other international students. Although its accreditation was revoked in 1949, it was regained in 1957. In 1993, the institution changed its name to DSU. It is one of the country's first land grant educational university rooted early-on in agriculture and education. DSU's focus on cutting-edge research in technology and business practices has brought the university into modem standards and made it a member of the scientific solution seeking community.

Relevant Information

Established: 1891

Type: Public, HBCU

Located: 1200 N Dupont Hwy., Dover, DE 19901

Phone: 302-857-6351

Religious Affiliation: NA

Student Enrollment: 4,425

Tuition Fees: In-state $7,336; out-of-state $15,692 Academic Staff: 436

Campus: Suburban, 400 acres

School Colors: Cherry red and Columbia blue

Mascot/Nickname: Hornets

Athletics/Sports Affiliations: NCAA Div. I, MEAC

Endowment: $20.8 million

Notable Alumni

Reggie Barnes: Canadian Football League running back.

Clyde Bishop: US Ambassador to Marshall Islands.

Clifford Brown: trumpet virtuoso and composer.

George F. Budd: president of St. Cloud State University, Kansas State College, and Pittsburgh State University.

Emanuel Davis: former NBA player.

Wayne Gilchrest: US Representative for Maryland Congressional District.

Jamaal Jackson: NFL player for Philadelphia Eagles.

Maxine A. Lewis: publicist in ABC TV.

Robert London: NFL sports agent.

Quincy A. Lucas: advocate against domestic violence and speaker.

Shaheer McBride: NFL and UFL player.

Damer McCants: NFL player.

Marlene Saunders: Delaware social worker and historian.

Harley F. Taylor: housing developer.

John Taylor: NFL player for San Francisco 49ers.

Bonsu Thompson: editor-in-chief of *Source* magazine.

Walter Tullis: NFL player for the Green Bay Packers.

David G. Turner: executive of Bank of America.

Ralph Wesley: public address announcer for Washington *Wizards*.

DENMARK TECHNICAL COLLEGE

History

Denmark Technical College is a two-year college located in Denmark, SC, and primarily serves Bamberg, Barnwell, and Allendale Counties in South Carolina. The school, which is state-supported, was established in 1947 as the South Carolina Area Trade School and offered courses in fields such as natural sciences, business and secretarial sciences, building sciences (carpentry, painting, plumbing, brick masonry, electrical sciences), air-conditioning and refrigeration, barbering and cosmetology; auto mechanics, shoe repair, and seamstress sciences and tailoring. Its sports teams were known as "The SCATS." The alumni of the South Carolina Area Trade School have established successful business across the United States.

Relevant Information

Established: 1947

Type: Public, HBCU

Location: 1126 Southern Blatt Blvd., Denmark, SC 29042

Phone: 803-793-5176

Religious Affiliation: NA

Student Enrollment: 2,238

Tuition Fees: In-state $2,594; out-of-state $4,874

Academic Staff: NA

Campus: Rural, 53 acres

School Colors: blue and white

Mascot/Nickname: Scats

Athletics/Sports Affiliation: NJCA

Endowment: $1.21 cents/student

Notable Alumni

J. A. Brown: nationally known comedian.

John S. Goodwin: president and CEO of Good Food Service, Inc.

James E. Byrd: owner and manager of Byrd's TV, Furniture, Appliance, Service and Rental Stores.

DILLARD UNIVERSITY

History

D illard University is a private, historically black, liberal arts college in New Orleans, LA. Found in 1930, incorporating earlier institutions that went back to 1869, it is affiliated with the United Church of Christ and the United Methodist Church. The campus is near Gentilly Boulevard and the London Avenue Canal and was founded in the 1930s. The history of Dillard dates back to 1869 and its founding predecessor institutions: Straight University (later to be named Straight College) and Union Normal School (which was to become New Orleans University). Due to economic hardship and rounds of negotiations between the two schools, the schools chartered Dillard University in 1930, offering a traditional liberal arts curriculum. Due to racial sensibilities, Dillard University opened its doors in the fall of 1935 and was able to attract a number of prominent scholars such as Horace Mann Bond, psychologist and educator; Lawrence Reddick, historian; and St. Clair Drake, sociologist and anthropologist.

Relevant Information

Established: 1869

Type: Private, HBCU

Location: 2601 Gentilly Blvd., New Orleans, LA 70122

Phone: 504-283-8822

Religious Affiliation: United Church of Christ and United Methodist Church

Student Enrollment: 1,307

Tuition Fees: In-state and out-of-state $13,650 Academic Staff: NA

Campus: Urban, 55 acres

School Colors: Royal blue and white

Mascot/Nickname: Blue Devils

Athletics/Sports Affiliations: GCAC and NAIA

Endowment: $45 million

Notable Alumni

James W. Ames: founder of Dunbar Hospital, Detroit, Ml.

William Banks: professor of African American studies, University of California at Berkeley.

Harold Battiste Jr.: jazz saxophonist, composer, and arranger.

Samuel L. Biggers: chief of neurosurgery at King/Drew Medical Center, Los Angeles.

John W. Brown: first African American to receive a PhD.

Jericho Brown: award-winning poet.

Cora N. Charles: lead-grant writer in developing the La. Genetics Disorder Division in Los Angeles.

Sherman Copelin: member of Louisiana House of Representatives.

Karen Drake: perinatologist, Iowa Methodist Medical Center.

Joseph N. Gayles: former president of Talladega College.

Sandra Hooker: associate dean of research at Morehouse School of Medicine.

Francis C. Henderson: professor of medicine and special assistant to the director of Jackson Heart Study.

Warren Jones: first African American elected president of the American Academy of Family Physicians.

Michael Jones: partner in Kirkland & Ellis; Georgetown Law Center Alumni of the Year awardee.

Harold Lundy Sr.: fourth president of GSU.

Larry Lund: president of Lundy Enterprises.

Glenda M. Goodly: senior vice president of American Express Co.

Ellis M. Marsalis: accomplished jazz pianist and father of jazz artists: Branford, Wynton, Jason, and Delfeayo.

Garrett Morris: comedian/actor.

Khalid A. Muhammad: national spokesman, Nation of Islam.

Alice D. Nelson: women rights activist and wife of Paul Lawrence Dunbar.

Alfred L. Norris: bishop of United Methodist Church.

Revius Orlique Jr.: first African American to serve on Louisiana State Supreme Court.

Brenda M. Osbey: poet Laureate.

Lisa F. Page: staff writer in *Washington Post*.

Louis Pendleton: dentist, businessman, and civic leader.

P. B. S. Pinchback: first African American governor in the United States and twenty-fourth governor of Louisiana.

Renee G. Pratt: New Orleans politician.

Beah Richards: actress of stage, screen, and TV and author and playwright.

Joyce M. Roche: president and CEO of Girls Inc.

John Ruffin: first associate director for Research on Minority Health and Disparities.

Ruth Simmons: first African American president of an Ivy League University (Brown University).

Mitchell W. Spellman: founding dean of Charles R. Drew University of Science and Medicine.

Rodrick A. Stevenson: director of Organ Transplant Department, Meharry Medical College.

Carl E. Stewart: judge of US 5th Circuit Court of Appeals in Louisiana.

William W. Sutton: fourth president of MVSU.

Dwayne Thomas: CEO of Medical Center in Louisiana, New Orleans.

Veronica White: former director of Sanitation for City of New Orleans.

Jimmy Womack: minster and member of Michigan House of Representatives.

UNIVERSITY OF THE DISTRICT OF COLUMBIA

History

The University of the District of Columbia (UDC) is a public university and was created in 1977 from the merger of the District of Columbia Teachers College with Federal City College and the Washington Technical Institute. In 1966, the District of Columbia Public Education Act created the Federal City College as a four-year liberal arts school and Washington Technical Institute was established as a technical school. Efforts to unify the D.C. Teachers College, Federal City College, Washington Technical Institute under a single administrative structure began in earnest after the passage of the District of Columbia Home Rule Act. A merger of the institutions was approved in 1975, and in August 1977, the three institutions were formally merged as the UDC, with Lisle Carter Jr. as its first president.

Relevant Information

Established: 1977

Type: Public, HBCU

Location: 4200 Connecticut Ave., NW, Washington, D.C. 20008

Phone: 202-274-5000

Religious Affiliation: NA

Student Enrollment: 5,137

Tuition Fees: In-state $4,147; out-of-state $7,267

Academic Staff: 1,099

Campus: Urban-Commuter, 23 acres

School Colors: Red and gold

Mascot/Nickname: Firebirds

Athletics/Sports Affiliation: NCAA Div. II

Endowment: $21.8 million

Notable Alumni

Denis G. Antoine: ambassador of Granada to the United States.

Thelma Thompson: president of the UMES.

Richard Pennington: chief of police, Atlanta, GA.

Norma H. Johnson: former US Federal judge.

Lennox Yearwood: president of Hip Hop Caucus.

Kali Troy: voice actress.

Aldon L. Nielsen: poet.

Cathy L. Lanier: chief of police, District of Columbia.

Branislav Andjeli: Serbian Internet pioneer, economist, and politician.

Lyn Mclain: cofounder of DC Youth Orchestra Program.

Carolyn Harris: library conservationist.

Rasheim Wright: Jordanian basketball player.

EDWARD WATERS COLLEGE

History

Edward Waters College is a private college located in Jacksonville, FL. It was founded in 1866 to educate freed former slaves and is the oldest historically black college in Florida. It is affiliated with the AME Church and is a part of the Independent Colleges and Universities of Florida. The first AME pastor in the state originally named the college Brown Theological Institute. Over the next 10 years, the curriculum was expanded, and the school was renamed after the third bishop of the AME Church. Edward Waters was accredited as a junior college, and in 1955, it had a restructured four-year curriculum. In 1979, the school was accredited as a four-year institution by the Commission on Colleges of the SACS and started awarding bachelor's degrees. After going through accreditation problems over several years, the college and SACS agreed to a settlement that allowed the reaffirmation of the college.

Relevant Information

Established: 1866

Type: Private, HBCU

Location: 1658 Kings Rd., Jacksonville, FL 32209

Phone: 904-470-8000

Religious Affiliation: AME Church

Student Enrollment: 800

Tuition Fees: $10,994

Academic Staff: NA

Campus: Urban, 50 acres

School Colors: Purple, orange, and white

Mascot/Nickname: Tigers

Athletics/Sports Affiliation: NAIA

Endowment: $1.6 million

Notable Alumni

Jim "Cannonball" Butler: former NFL running back.

Reggie Brown: Jacksonville City Council Representative.

Nathaniel Glover: president of Edward Waters College and former sheriff of Jacksonville.

Betty Holzendorf: former Florida State Representative.

Fredrick D. Harper: author and scholar.

Buck O'Heil: former Negro League baseball player.

Rahman Johnson: TV personality, actor, and former Duval County commissioner.

ELIZABETH CITY STATE UNIVERSITY

History

ECSU is a public, historically black college located in Elizabeth City, NC. It is a member-school of the Thurgood Marshall College Fund. ECSU was established by the North Carolina General Assembly in 1891 to a bill calling schools of North Carolina. In 1937, the school made the transformation into a full four-year teachers college and was officially named Elizabeth City State Teachers College. In 1961, the college gained membership in the SACS. In 1963, its name was changed to Elizabeth City State College and in 1969 its name was changed to Elizabeth City State University to reflect expansion and the addition of graduate programs. When the University of North Carolina System was formed in 1972, ECSU became one of the system's sixteen consultant universities and entered into its current phase of development and organization.

Relevant Information

Established: 1891

Type: Public, HBCU

Location: 1704 Weeksville Rd., Elizabeth City, NC 27909

Phone: 252-335-3400

Religious Affiliation: NA

Student Enrollment: 2,836

Tuition Fees: In-state $4,151; out-of-state $13,894

Academic Staff: NA

Campus: Rural, 200 acres

School Colors: Royal blue and white

Mascot/Nickname: Vikings

Athletics/Sports Affiliation: NCAA, CIAA Div. II

Endowment: $4,286,497

Notable Alumni

Reggie Langhorne: former NFL wide receiver.

Larry Johnson Sr.: former NFL linebacker, current defensive line coach at Penn State University.

Jethro Pugh: former NFL defensive tackle.

Mike Gale: former professional basketball player in both the ABA and the NBA.

Johnnie Walton: former NFL quarterback with the Philadelphia Eagles and the Boston Breakers of the USFL.

Ronald M. Leigh Sr.: former NFL defensive end with the New England Patriots.

Everett McIver: former NFL offensive guard.

Bobby Futrell: former NFL defensive back.

Tim Cofield: former NFL and CFL linebacker.

Kenny Williams: former professional basketball player.

FAYETTEVILLE STATE UNIVERSITY

History

The institution that would become Fayetteville State University and be recognized as the second oldest, state-supported school in North Carolina had humble beginnings. In 1865, a robust education agenda was begun in Fayetteville's African American community with the founding of the Phillips and Summer Schools for primary and intermediate learning. Soon after, in 1867, these schools were merged to form Howard School. In 1877, an act of the North Carolina Legislature provided for the establishment of a teacher training institution for African Americans in the state. Recognized for its success in educating black youth, the Howard School became the State Colored Normal School. Later, in 1939, the school became Fayetteville State Teachers College. In 1969, the school was renamed Fayetteville State University as a constituent institution of the University of North Carolina System.

Relevant Information

Established: 1867

Type: Public, HBCU

Location: 1200 Murchison Rd., Fayetteville, NC 28301

Phone: 910-672-1111

Religious Affiliation: NA

Student Enrollment: 5,930

Tuition Fees: Various, from $11,389 to $26,000

Academic Staff: 328

Campus: Urban, 200 acres

School Colors: White and blue

Mascot/Nickname: Broncos

Athletics/Sports Affiliation: NCAA Div. II, CIAA

Endowment: $15.1 million

Notable Alumni

Jerry C. Johnson: former head basketball coach at LeMoyne-Owen College and second winningest couch in Div. II, NCAA history.

Chris Armstrong: former professional football player in Canadian Football League.

Darrell Armstrong: former professional basketball player.

Jim Bibby: former MLB player.

Sylvester Ritter: former NFL player and professional wrestler (known as "Junk Yard Dog").

Richard Medlin: NFL player for Miami Dolphins and Atlanta Falcons.

Affion Crockett: actor, writer, dancer, rapper, comedian, and music producer.

FISK UNIVERSITY

History

Fisk University is a historically black university founded in 1866 in Nashville, TN. The *40-acre* campus is a historic district listed on the National Register of Historic Places. Fisk was the first African American institution to gain accreditation by the SACS. In 1952, Fisk was the first predominantly black college to earn National Honor Society's Phi Beta Kappa charter. The chapter inducted its first student members in 1953. In 1866, the Fisk Free Colored School was founded for the education of freedmen, with ages of students ranging from seven to seventy. The school was named in honor of Gen. Clinton B. Fisk of the Tennessee Freedmen's Bureau, who made unused barracks available to the school as well as establishing the first free schools for white and black children in Tennessee. The AMA's work was supported by the United Church of Christ, which retains an affiliation with the university. In 2008, Fisk announced that it had successfully raised $4 million during the fiscal year as it faced significant financial hardship and claimed that it may need to dose its doors unless its finances improve.

Relevant Information

Established: 1866

Type: Private, HBCU

Location: 1000 17th Ave., North, Nashville, TN 37208

Phone: 615-329-8500

Religious Affiliation: United Church of Christ

Student Enrollment: 800

Tuition Fees: In-state and out-of-state $20,391

Academic Staff: 70

Campus: Urban, 42 acres

School Colors: Blue and gold

Mascot/nickname: Bulldogs

Athletics/Sports Affiliations: NCAA, SACS

Endowment: $13,438,891

Notable Alumni

Lil H. Armstrong: jazz pianist/composer and second wife of Louis Armstrong.

Constance B. Motley: first African American woman elected to the New York state senate.

Marion Barry: former mayor of Washington, D.C.

Mary F. Berry: former chair of US Commission on Civil Rights and former chancellor of University of Colorado at Boulder.

John Betsch: jazz percussionist.

Joyce Bolden: first African American woman to serve in the Commission for Accreditation of the National Association of Schools of Music.

Otis Boykin: inventor of control device for the heart pacemaker.

St. E Brady: first African American to earn a doctorate in chemistry.

Cora Brown: first African American woman elected as a state senate.

Henry A. Cameron: educator, decorated World War I veteran.

J. O. Patterson Jr.: first African American mayor of Memphis, Memphis state senator, and bishop in the Church of God in Christ.

Elizabeth H. Canady: past president of Delta Sigma Theta sorority.

Alfred O. Coffin: first African American to earn a doctorate in zoology.

Johnnetta B. Cole: anthropologist and former president of Spelman College and Bennett College.

William L. Dawson: US Congressman.

Arthur Cunningham: music composer, studied at Julliard University.

Charles Digg: US House of Representatives, Michigan.

Mahala A. Dickerson: first black female attorney in the state of Alabama and president of National Association of Women Lawyers.

W. E. B. Du Bois: sociologist, scholar, first African American to earn a PhD from Harvard University.

Venida Evans: actress, best known for IKEA commercials.

Etta Z. Falconer: First African American to receive a PhD in mathematics.

John Hope Franklin: historian, professor, scholar, and author.

Victor O. Frazer: member of the US House of Representatives.

Alonzo Fulgham: former acting chief and operating officer of the US Agency for International Development.

Nikki Giovanni: poet, author, professor, and scholar.

Louis G. Gregory: Hand of the Cause in Bahai Faith.

Alcee Hastings: US congressman and former US District Court judge.

Roland Hayes: concert singer.

Perry W. Howard: assistant US Attorney General under President Herbert Hoover.

Elmer Imes: renowned physicist and second African American to earn a Ph.D. in Physics.

Esther C. Jackson: founding editor of *Freedomways* journal.

Leonard Jackson: actor in films *Five on the Black Hand Side* and *The Color Purple.*

Robert James: former NFL cornerback.

Judith Jamison: pioneering dancer and choreographer and former artistic director of Alvin Ailey American Dance Theater.

Ted Jarrett: R&B recording artist and producer.

Charles Jeter: father of Derek Jeter.

Ben Jobe: legendary basketball coach of Southern University.

Lewis W. Jones: sociologist; Julius Rosenwald Foundation Fellow at Columbia University.

Ella M. Johnson: At the age of 105 years, she traveled to Washington, D.C., to attend the inauguration of President Barack Obama.

Matthew Knowles: father and manager of Beyoncé Knowles.

Nella Larsen: novelist, Harlem Renaissance Era

Julius Lester: author of Children's books.

David L. Lewis: two-time Pulitzer Prize winner.

John Lewis: congressman, civil rights activist and former president of Student Nonviolent Coordinating Committee.

Jimmie Lunceford: Famous bandleader in the Swing Era.

Aubrey Lyles: Vaudville performer.

E. M. Lysonge: former SGA president and currently serves as vice president of Legal Affairs at Churchill Downs Incorporated.

Mandisa: Grammy and Dove Award singer/songwriter.

Patti J. Malone: Fisk Jubilee singer.

Louis E. Martin: godfather of black politics.

Wade H. McCree: second African American US Solicitor General and justice of US Court of Appeals for Sixth Circuit.

Samuel A. McElwee: state senator during the Reconstruction Era.

Robert A. McFerrin: first African American to sing at the Metropolitan

Opera and father of Bobby McFerrin.

Leslie Meek: administrative law judge and wife of Congressman Kendrick Meek.

Ronald E. Mickens: physicist and winner of the Edward Bouchet Award.

Theo Mitchell: senator of South Carolina General Assembly.

Undine S. Moore: received scholarship to Julliard.

Diane Nash: founding member of SNCC.

Rachel B. Noel: politician and first African American to serve on Denver Public School Board of Education.

Hazel O'Leary: former US Secretary of Energy and President of Fisk University.

Helen Phillips: first African American to perform with the Metropolitan Opera chorus.

Annette L. Phinazee: first black woman to earn a doctorate in library sciences from Columbia University.

Anita Ponder: partner of Drinker Biddle & Reath LLC and lawyers.

Alma Power: wife of Gen. Colin Powell.

Kay G. Roberts: orchestral conductor.

Bradley T. Sheares: former CEO of Reliant Pharmaceuticals and former president of H.H. Division in Merck & Co.

Martha L. Sherrod: presiding District Court judge in North Alabama.

Lorenzo D. Turner: linguist and chair of African Studies at Roosevelt University.

A. Maceo Walker: businessman, Universal Life Insurance, Tri-State Bank.

Ron Walters: scholar of African American politics and chair of Afro-American Studies at Brandeis University.

Margaret M. Washington: lady principal of Tuskegee Institute and third wife of Booker T. Washington.

Ida B. Wells: American civil rights activist and women's suffrage advocate.

Charles H. Wesley: president of Wilberforce University and president of

Central State College and third African American to receive a PhD from Harvard.

Kym Whitley: actress and comedienne.

Frederica Wilson: US Representative for Florida.

Tom Wilson: music producer, best known for his work with Bob Dylan and Frank Zappa.

Yetta Young: first to produce all African American celebrity cast of the Obie-Award winning play *The Vagina Monologues*.

Frank Yerby: first African American to publish a best-selling novel.

FLORIDA A&M UNIVERSITY

History

Florida A&M University—commonly known as Florida A&M or FAMU—is a public, historically black university in Tallahassee, FL. Founded in 1887, it is the largest historically black university in the United States by enrollment. It is a member institution of the State University of Florida, as well as one of the state's land-grant universities, and is accredited to award baccalaureate, master's and doctoral degrees by the Commission on Colleges of the SACS. The university is a member of the Thurgood Marshall College Fund. It offers 62 bachelor's degrees in 103 majors/tracks. Thirty-six master's degrees with fifty-six majors/tracks are offered within eleven of the university's thirteen schools and colleges. Two professional degrees and eleven PhD degrees are offered. Although Florida A&M has been accredited by the SACS since 1935, it is currently on probation following "a series of scandals."

Relevant Information

Established: 1887

Type: Public, HBCU

Location: 1700 S. Adams St., Tallahassee, Fl 32301

Phone: 850-599-3000

Religious Affiliation: NA

Student Enrollment: 13,089

Tuition Fees: In-state $5,187; out-of-state $17,127

Academic Staff: 620

Campus: Urban, 420 acres

School Colors: Orange and green

Mascot/Nickname: Rattlers

Athletics/Sports Affiliations: NCAA, MEAC Div. I

Endowment: $88 million

Notable Alumni

Kimberlee D. Borland: Miss Black Universe (2007).

Andre Harper: political analyst and author.

Bernard Kinsey: owner of one of the largest African American art collections.

Julian "Cannonball" Adderley: jazz alto saxophonist.

Nate Adderley: jazz cornetist.

Common: rapper and entertainer.

Clayton Gavin: member of hip-hop group Dead Prez.

Mutulu Olugabala: member of hip-hop group Dead Prez. Smitty: rapper and producer.

Rico Love: rapper and songwriter.

Tabi Bonney: rapper.

Norris "NG" Garganious: member of R&B group Unit 4.

Ronnie Mackey: member of R&B group Unit 4.

K. Michelle: R&B singer.

Keyah C. Keymah: activist.

Pam Oliver: sports anchor.

Anika Rose: Tony Award-winning actress.

Meshach Taylor: actor.

William Packer: film producer.

Rob Hardy: film producer.

Gregory Anderson: film producer.

Daniel Sunjata: Broadway actor.

Angela Pitts: winner of "I Love Money 2."

Motown Maurice: Late Night Talk Show host.

Roy Woods: comedian and radio personality.

Corrine Brown: US Congresswoman.

Wilkie D. Ferguson: former judge of US District Court of Florida.

Andrew Gillum: city commissioner of Tallahassee.

Kwame Kilpatrick: former mayor of Detroit.

Lemuel Geathers: first black mayor of Winter Haven, FL.

Alfred Lawson: member of Florida senate.

Alcea L. Hastings: US Congressman.

Mia L. Jones: member of Florida House of Representatives.

Jesse J. McCrary: lawyer, civil rights activist, and former secretary of state of Florida.

Kendrick Meek: former US Congressman.

Carrie P. Meek: former US Congressman.

Gwendolyn M. Miller: chairwoman of city council, Tampa, FL.

Alzo J. Reddick: former member of the Florida House of Representatives.

David Scott: US Representative of Georgia's 13th district.

John W. Williams: inspector general of South Florida Water Management District.

Robert Guthrie: psychologist and author.

LaSalle D. Leffal: nationally acclaimed cancer surgeon.

Arthur R. Collins: president and CEO of public-private partnership.

Raymond Brown: nationally known attorney.

John Thompson: chairman and former president and CEO of Symantec Corporation and part owner of Golden State Warriors.

Gene Atkins: NFL football player.

Greg Coleman: NFL football player.

Jamie Brown: NFL football player.

Hewritt Dixon: NFL football player.

Glen Edwards: NFL football player.

Kevin Elliott: NFL football player.

Willie Galimore: NFL football player.

Quinn Gray: NFL football player.

Earl Homes: NFL football player.

Roosevelt Kiser: NFL football player.

Henry Lawrence: NFL football player.

Terry Mickens: NFL football player.

Dexter Nottage: NFL football player.

Nate Newton: NFL football player.

Jamie Nails: NFL football player.

Dan Parish: NFL football player.

Ken Riley: NFL football player.

Wally Williams: NFL football player.

Vince Colenan: MLB player.

Marquis Grissom: MLB player.

Althea Gibson: tennis player.

Casey Printers: CFL player.

FLORIDA MEMORIAL UNIVERSITY

History

Florida Memorial University is a private, coeducational, four-yearn university located in Miami Gardens, FL. It is one of the thirty-nine member institutions of the UNCF and a historically black, Baptist-related institution which is ranked second in Florida and ninth in the United States for graduating African American teachers. The university was founded in 1879 as the Florida Baptist Institute in Live Oak, FL. With the support of the American Baptist Home Mission Society, the first regular school year began in 1880. In 1882, the Florida Baptist Academy was established in Jacksonville, FL. The name was later changed to Florida Normal and Industrial Institute. It was there that two brothers, James Weldon Johnson and J. Rosamond, wrote the words and music to "Lift Every Voice and Sing," which is known as the Negro National Anthem. The school was moved to St. Augustine in 1918 on a 110-acre tract of land. The school's name was changed to Florida Normal and Industrial Memorial College and later changed to Florida Memorial College. In 2004, the name was changed to Florida Memorial University.

Relevant Information

Established: 1879

Type: Private, HBCU

Location: 15800 Northwest, 42nd Ave., Miami Gardens, FL 33054

Phone: 305-626-3600

Religious Affiliation: American Baptist Church USA

Student Enrollment: 1,800

Tuition Fees: $14,604

Academic Staff: NA

Campus: Urban, 44 acres

School Colors: Royal blue and orange

Mascot/Nickname: Lions

Athletics/Sports Affiliation: SIAC.

Endowment: $9.76 millions

Notable Alumni

Barrington Irving Jr.: first and youngest African American pilot to fly solo around the world.

Freddie L. Peterkin: soul and gospel singer.

Bishop V. T. Curry: pastor of New Birth Baptist Church in Miami, FL, and is on the board of trustees of Florida Memorial University.

FORT VALLEY STATE UNIVERSITY

History

Fort Valley State University (FVSU) is a historically black university located in Fort Valley, GA. It is a unit of the University System of Georgia and a member of the Thurgood Marshall College Fund. Fort Valley is approximately 100 miles south of Atlanta, GA, and 25 miles south of Macon, GA. FVSU, formerly Fort Valley State College, began with the 1939 merger of the Fort Valley High and Industrial School—chartered in 1895—and the State Teachers and Agricultural College of Forsyth. These schools were merged and became Fort Valley State College. In 1947, the State Board of Regents adopted a resolution moving the land-grant designation from Savannah State College to Fort Valley State College. In 1957, the college received full membership in the SACS, and in 1996, the school became FVSU, a state and land-grant university.

Relevant Information

Established: 1895

Type: Public, HBCU

Location: 1005 State University Dr., Fort Valley, GA 31030

Phone: 478-825-6223

Religious Affiliation: NA

Student Enrollment: 4,250

Tuition Fees: In-state $6,080; out-of-state $17,984

Academic Staff: 400

Campus: Rural, 1,365 acres

School Colors: Royal blue and old gold

Mascot/Nickname: Wildcats

Athletics/Sports Affiliation: SIAC

Endowment: $5,124,791

Notable Alumni

Lonnie Bartley: women's head basketball coach at FVSU.

John W. Blassingame: professor and chair of African Studies at Yale University for 29 years.

Alvin J. Copeland: athletic director and girls' high school basketball coach at Northeast Health Science Management High School.

Tommy Dortch: former president of 100 Black Men of America, Inc.

Nick Harper: former NFL cornerback for Tennessee Titans and Indianapolis Colts.

Samuel D. Jolly: fourteenth president of MBC.

Marquette King: NFL punter for the Oakland Raiders.

Genevieve M. Knight: educator and recipient of Outstanding Faculty Award from White House Initiative on HBCU.

Ricardo Lockette: NFL wide receiver for Seattle Seahawks and San Francisco 49ers.

Greg Lloyd: former NFL Pro Bowl player for Pittsburgh Steelers.

L. J. "Stan" Lomax: head football coach at Fort Valley State and inducted into Georgia Sports Hall of Fame.

Tyrone Poole: earned 2 Super Bowl rings with New England Patriots. Peppi Zellner: former NFL player.

Derrick Wimbush: former NFL player.

Charles Robinson Jr.: president and CEO of Sadie G. Mays Health and Rehabilitation Center in Atlanta.

Calvin Smyre: elected to Georgia House of Representatives.

Peyton Williams Jr.: highest ranking African American official in the US Department of Education for 25 years.

Rayfield Wright: NFL Hall of Fame inductee.

GADSDEN STATE COMMUNITY COLLEGE

History

G adsden State Community College is a two-year institution of higher learning located in Gadsden, Anniston, and Centre, AL. The college's service area takes in Calhoun, Cherokee, Cleburne, Etowah, and parts of St. Clair Counties. The college underwent some turmoil in 2013 when the majority members of the faculty and staff voted no confidence in the president, Ray Staats. He was replaced on leave as an interim was appointed. The college has four campuses and two centers: the Wallace Drive Campus, the East Broad Campus, the Ayers Campus, the Valley Street Campus, the McClellan Center, and the Gadsden State Cherokee Center. The college is accredited by the Commission on Colleges of the SACS.

Relevant Information

Established: 1925

Type: Public, HBUC

Location: 1001 George Wallace Dr., Gadsden, AL 35903

Phone: 256-549-8200

Religious Affiliation: NA

Student Enrollment: 8,000

Tuition Fees: $10,704 annually

Academic Staff: 490

Campus: Medium size

School Colors: Red and white

Mascot/Nickname: Cardinals

Athletics/Sports Affiliation: ACCC

Endowment: NA

Notable Alumni

NA

GRAMBLING STATE UNIVERSITY

History

GSU is a historically black, public, coeducational university, located in Grambling, LA. The university is the home of the late head coach Eddie Robinson and is listed on the Louisiana African Heritage Trail. The university is a member-school of the Thurgood Marshall College Fund. Grambling State was founded in 1901 and accredited in 1949.

The school became Grambling College in 1946, gaining university status in 1974. The North Louisiana Colored Agriculture Relief Association was formed to organize and operate a school. After opening the school in the town of Grambling, the association requested assistance from Booker T. Washington of Tuskegee Institute of Alabama to aid the group in organizing an industrial school. Four years later, the school moved to its present location and was named the North Louisiana Agricultural and Industrial School. The institution's name was changed in 1946 in honor of a white sawmill owner, P. G. Grambling. In 1974, the addition of graduate programs in early childhood and elementary education gave the school a new status and a new name called GSU.

Relevant Information

Established: 1901

Type: Pubic, HBCU

Location: 403 Main St., Grambling, LA 71245

Phone: 318-247-3811

Religious Affiliation: NA

Student Enrollment: 4,994

Tuition Fees: In-state out-of-state $14,584

Academic Staff: NA

Campus: Rural, 384 acres

School Colors: Black and gold

Mascot/Nickname: Tigers

Athletics/Sports Affiliations: SWAG, NCAA Div. II

Endowment: $4.5 million

Notable Alumni

Willie Brown: NFL player of Green Bay Packers.

Ronnie Coleman: Olympia winner.

Natalie D. Reid: actress.

Erykah Badu: Grammy winner.

Charles M. Blow: *New York Times* columnist.

Pinkie C. Wilkerson: member of Louisiana House of Representatives.

Doug Williams: Super Bowl star.

Ahmad Terry: photographer and Pulitzer Prize winner.

Stephanie Finley: nominated as US Attorney for Louisiana.

Michael Thomas: renowned jazz artist.

Lovett Hines: jazz artist.

Judi-Ann Mason: writer.

N. Burl Cain: warden of Louisiana state penitentiary.

HAMPTON UNIVERSITY

History

Hampton University is a historically black and Native American university located in Hampton, VA. It was founded by black and white leaders of the AMA after the American Civil War to provide education to freedmen. The AMA responded in 1861 to the former slaves' need for education by hiring its first mulatto teacher, Mary Smith Peake, who had secretly been teaching slaves and free blacks in the area despite the state's prohibition law. She gathered her pupils under a large oak in 1863 and read the first reading in the South of the Emancipation Proclamation. It was called the Emancipation Oak, which is part of the National Landmark District at Hampton University. The Hampton Agricultural and Industrial School, later called Hampton Institute, was founded in 1868 after the war by the biracial leadership of the AMA, who was chiefly Congregational and Presbyterian ministers. After the Civil War, a normal school was formalized in 1868 with former Union brevet Brigadier General Samuel Chapman Armstrong (1838-1893) as its first principal. Hampton Normal and Agricultural Institute became simply Hampton Institute in 1930, and in 1984, it was accredited as Hampton University.

Relevant Information

Established: 1868

97

Type: Private, HBCU

Location: 100 East Queen St., Hampton, VA 23668

Phone: 757-727-5000

Religious Affiliation: AMA

Student Enrollment: 5,000

Tuition Fees: $19,738

Academic Staff: NA

Campus: Suburban, 314 acres

School Colors: Blue and white

Mascot/Nickname: Pirates

Athletics/Sports affiliation: NCAA, MEAC Div. 8

Endowment: $240,013,666

Notable Alumni

Vanessa D. Gilmore: federal judge of US District Court.

Theodore T. Jones: associate judge of the Court of Appeals, New York.

Gloria G. Lawlah: secretary of Aging for the State of Maryland.

F. Chris Lee: member, city council, Tuskegee, AL.

Bryan T. Norwood: police chief of Richmond police station, Virginia.

Douglas Palmer: mayor of Trenton, New Jersey.

Henry E. Parker: former state treasurer of Connecticut.

Joan Pratt: comptroller of City of Baltimore.

Gregory M. Sleet: US district judge.

Charles Phillips: CEO of Infor and former president of Oracle Corporation.

Tami Simmons: senior vice president of Wells Fargo.

Booker T. Washington: founded Tuskegee Institute.

John A. Kenney: secretary of National Medical Association.

Martha L. M. Foxx: notable blind educator.

St. Clair Drake: notable sociologist and anthropologist.

Freeman A. Hrabowski: president of the University of Maryland, Baltimore County.

Kimberly Oliver: National Teacher of the Year 2006.

William C. Hunter: dean of the Tippie College of Business, University of Iowa.

Wilmer Leon: political scientist and associate professor at Howard University.

Ezrah Aharone: political and economic consultant and a scholar of Sovereign Studies.

Dianne B. Suber: president of Saint Augustine's College.

Edward McIntosh: scholar and educator.

Roberts Ferrell: major general of US Army.

W.C. Weddington: member of Ohio House of Representatives.

Spencer Overton: electronic scholar of George Washington University Law School.

Alberta Williams King: mother of Martin Luther King Jr.

Elizabeth Omilami: chief executive officer of the Hosea Freed the Hungry and Homeless.

Darian Barnes: NFL running back, Tampa Bay Buccaneers.

Johnnie Barnes: NFL wide receiver.

James Carter: award-winning track athlete.

Marcus Dixon: NFL football player of the Dallas Cowboys and New York Jets.

Justin Durant: NFL football player of the Detroit Lions.

Kendrick Ellis: NFL football player of the New York Jets.

Devin Green: former NBA player.

Rick Mahom: Former NBA player of Washington Bullets, Detroit Pistons, and New Jersey Jets.

Nevin McCaskill: former NFL football player.

Francena McCorory: track and field, NCAA 400m champion.

Kellie Wells: track and field sprinter.

Marquay McDaniel: CFL football player, Hamilton Tiger-Cats.

Dick Price: former head football and track coach at NSU and athletic director.

Donovan Rose: former NFL defensive back and head coach of Hampton's football team.

Terrence Warren: Seattle Seahawks football player.

Cordell Taylor: Jacksonville Jaguars football player.

Jerome Mathis: drafted by Houston Texans of 2005 Pro Bowl selection

Isaac Hilton: New Giants football player.

John T. Biggers: Harlem Renaissance Muralist and founder of the Arts Department at TSU.

Spencer Christian: former weatherman for *Good Morning America*.

Wanda Sykes: comedian.

D. J. Envy: disc jockey.

Kenneth L. Riddle: recording artist and member of Tye Tribbett and Greater Anointing.

Robi Reed: casting director of *School Daze*, *Love Jones*, and *Soul Food*. Dorothy Maynor: concert singer.

Brandon Fobbs: actor, who acted in the movie *Pride* with Terrence Howard.

Beverly Gooden: best-selling author, *Confessions of a Church Girl*.

Emil Wilbekin: entertainment journalist, former editor-in-chief for *Vibe* magazine.

Angela B. Murray: editor-in-chief of *Essence* magazine.

Biff Henderson: stage manager and personality on the Late Show with

David Letterman.

A. S. (Doc) Young: sports journalist.

Allyson K. Duncan: US Circuit Court judge.

Michael K. Fauntroy: professor of public policy at Georgia Mason University and political commentator.

James Griffin: football quarterback at Hampton Institute.

Robert Saeen: head tennis coach at Hampton Institute and Hampton University.

Wallace Hooker: six-sport letterman at Hampton Institute.

George Williams: matchless javelin thrower at Hampton Institute.

Alphonso W. Knight: all-time great basketball player at H. I. and CIAA pole vault champion in 1947.

Maurice Jones: CIM heavy weight boxing champion during the 1940s.

Thomas Casey: H.I. football great, doctor, professional football player, and scholar.

HARRIS-STOWE STATE UNIVERSITY

History

H arris-Stowe State University is a historically black, public university located in midtown St. Louis, MO. The university is a member school of the Thurgood Marshall College Fund. Founded in 1857, Harris-Stowe State University is one of the oldest institutions of higher education in Missouri. Founded by the St. Louis Public Schools as a normal school, it was the first public teacher education institution west of the Mississippi River and the twelfth such institution in the United States. During most of this period, the emphasis focused on teacher education: however, the state senate enacted a bill in 1993 enhancing the mission of Harris-Stowe to include a wider selection of degree opportunities. Harris-Stowe State University was called Harris-Stowe State College until it was renamed in 2005.

Relevant Information

Established: 1857

Type: Public, HBCU

Location: 3026 Laclede Ave., St. Louis, MO 63103

Phone: 314-340-3366

Religious Affiliation: NA

Student Enrollment: 1,716

Tuition Fees: In-state $4,553; out-of-state $8,562

Academic Staff: NA

Campus: Urban, 31 acres

School Colors: Brown and gold

Mascot/Nickname: Hornets

Athletics/Sports Affiliation: NAIA, AMC

Endowment: NA

Notable Alumni

David S. Cunningham Jr.: city councilmember of Los Angeles, CA.

Paul Hibbler: stand-up comedian and sports commentator.

Arlene Ackerman: former superintendent of Public Schools in Washington D.C., San Francisco, and Philadelphia.

Julius Hunter: retired TV anchorman and former St. Louis University vice president and author.

Bobby Wilks: US Coast Guard aviator and first African American promoted to the rank of captain in Coast Guard.

HINDS COMMUNITY COLLEGE

History

Hinds Community College is a community college with its main campus located in Raymond, MS., about 5 miles west of Jackson, the state capital. The Hinds Community College District includes Hinds County, Claiborne County, part of Copiah County, and Warren County. Utica Junior College, a historically black, junior college, merged with Hinds Junior College in 1982 under Federal Court order. Hinds Junior College changed its name to Hinds Community College in 1987 and thirteen of the fourteen other Mississippi public two-year colleges also adopted the "community" label. Hinds linked up with other two-year colleges by means of the Community College Network (CCN), allowing a course to be offered at one college location while students may participate in the course at several other college locations.

Relevant Information

Established: 1917

Type: Public, HBCU

Location: 3925 Sunset Dr., Jackson, MS 39213

Phone: 601-987-8107

Religious Affiliation: NA

Student Enrollment: 12,811

Tuition Fees: $14,328 per year

Academic Staff: NA

Campus: Urban/suburban and size: NA

School Colors: White and maroon

Mascot/Nickname: Eagles

Athletics/Sports Affiliation: MACJC and NJCAA

Endowment: NA

Notable Alumni

John B. Williams: Former governor of Mississippi.

Chad Bradford: MLB player.

Corey Bradford: NFL player.

Phil Bryant: sixty-fourth and current governor of Mississippi.

John Copeland: NFL player.

Beasley Denson: former tribal chief of the Mississippi Band of Choctaw Indians.

Faith Hill: country music singer. Grady Jackson: NFL player. Earl Leggett: NFL player.

Leon Lett: Dallas Cowboys Pro Bowl player.

Scott Mateer: former songwriter and radio disc jockey.

HOWARD UNIVERSITY

History

Howard University is a federally chartered, private, coeducational, nonsectarian, historically black university located in Washington, D.C. It is a high research institution open to people of both sexes and all races. Shortly after the end of the Civil War, members of the First Congregational Society of Washington considered establishing a theological seminary for the education of African American clergymen. Within a few weeks, the project expanded to include a provision for establishing a university.

Within two years, the university consisted of the College of Liberal Arts and Medicine. The new institution was named after Gen. Oliver Otis Howard, a Civil War hero, who was both the founder of the University and, at that time, the commissioner of the Freedmen's Bureau. Congress chartered Howard in 1867, and much of its early funding came from endowment, private benefaction, and tuition.

Relevant Information

Established: 1867

Type: Private, HBCU

Location: 2400 6th St. NW, Washington, D.C. 20059

Phone: 202-806-6100

Religious Affiliation: Former Theological school.

Student Enrollment: 10,000

Tuition Fees: $25,905

Academic Staff: NA

Campus: Urban, 500 acres

School Colors: Blue and white

Mascot/Nickname: Bisons

Athletics/Sports Affiliation: NCAA Div. I, MEAC

Endowment: $460.7 million

Notable Alumni

Ben Ali: cofounder and owner of Ben's Chili Bowl.

Debbie Allen: choreographer, actress, and singer.

Nnamdi Azikiwe: first Nigerian president.

Antoine Bethea: NFL football player.

Elijah Cummings: US Congressman.

Ossie Davis: actor.

Cheick M. Diarra: Malian prime minister and NASA engineer.

David Dinkins: first African American mayor of New York City.

Mike Espy: first African American US Secretary of Agriculture.

Adrian Fenty: former mayor of Washington, D. C.

Patricia R. Harris: former US Secretary of Housing and first African American woman US Ambassador.

Gus Johnson: American sports broadcaster.

Vernon Jordan: attorney.

Ananda Lewis: American TV personality.

Thurgood Marshall: former US Supreme Court justice.

Toni Morrison: Nobel Prize and Pulitzer Prize winner.

Phylicia Rashad: actress and singer.

Kasin Reed: mayor of Atlanta, GA.

Crystal Waters: American dance music singer and songwriter.

Andrew Young: former US Ambassador.

Stokely Carmichael (Kwame Toure): civil rights leader.

A. J. Calloway: TV personality.

HOUSTON-TILLOTSON UNIVERSITY

History

Houston-Tillotson University is a historically black college affiliated with the United Methodist Church, the United Church of Christ, and the UNCF. The university awards four-year degrees in business, education, humanities, natural and social sciences, and technology. Its history involves two schools: Tillotson College and Sam Houston College. In 1952, two colleges merged to become Houston-Tillotson University. It became Tillotson-Houston University in 2005. It is located at the site of the former Tillotson College on a land feature formerly known as Bluebonnet Hill and occupies a 24-acre campus. Before the merger, future baseball legend Jackie Robinson accepted an offer from his old friend and pastor Rev. Karl Downs, who was president of college, to be the athletic director of the college and then of the Southwestern Athletic Conference. Robinson was respected as a disciplinarian coach and drew the admiration of Langston University basketball player Marques Haynes, among others—a future member of the Harlem Globetrotters.

Relevant Information

Established: 1875

Type: Private, HBCU

Location: 900 Chicon St., Austin, TX 78702

Phone: 512-505-3000

Religious Affiliation: United Methodist Church of Christ

Student Enrollment: 900

Tuition Fees: $11,020

Academic Staff: NA

Campus: Urban, 24 acres

School Colors: Gold and maroon

Mascot/Nickname: Rams

Athletics/Sports Affiliation: NAIA, RRAC, SWAG

Endowment: $7 million

Notable Alumni

Herman Barnet: first African American to be admitted to the University of Texas Medical School.

Azie Taylor: treasurer of the United States during the Carter's administration.

Robert G. Stanton: former national director of US Park Service during Clinton's administration.

June H. Brewer: former educator and was among first five blacks to be admitted to the University of Texas.

Maceo T. Bowie: first president of the Kennedy-King City College in Chicago.

Karl E. Downs: minister in the United Methodist Church and former president of Huston-Tillotson University.

James A. Harris: scientist and identified elements 104 and 105.

Robert E. Hayes: bishop of the United Methodist Church and served as regional minister of congregations.

Cecil Williams: community leader, author, lecturer, and spokesperson for the poor.

Joe Leonard Jr.: assistant secretary for civil rights and former executive director of Congressional Black Caucus.

Alexander Howard: African American feminist studies theoretician.

Elizabeth Conley: Texas philanthropist and GLBTQ advocate.

Bobby Bradford: jazz trumpeter, cornetist, bandleader, and composer.

Bert Collins: former president of North Carolina Mutual Insurance Company.

INTERDENOMINATIONAL THEOLOGICAL CENTER

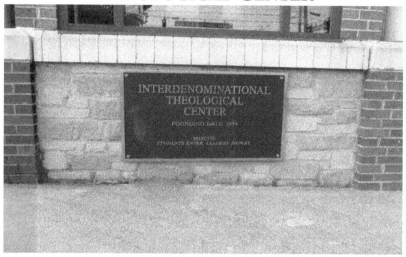

History

Interdenominational Theological Center of six predominantly AfricanAmerican seminaries (American Baptist Churches, USA; Baptist Convention, USA; and the Progressive National Baptist Convention), Gammon Theological Seminary (United Methodist), Turner Theological Seminary (AME), Phillip School of Theology (CME), Charles H. Mason Theological Seminary (Church of God in Christ), and Johnson C. Smith Theological Seminary (Presbyterian Church, USA). Their mission is to educate Christian leaders for ministry and service. The idea of a single collaborate institution for training and development of African American Christian ministers was spawned under Benjamin Mays when Morehouse College and Gammon Theological Seminary began a cooperative exchange program. The center is located in Atlanta, GA.

Relevant Information

Established: 1958

Type: Private, HBCU

Location: 700 Martin Luther King Jr. Dr. SW, Atlanta, GA 30314

Phone: 404- 527-7700

Religious Affiliation: Inter-denominations

Enrollment: 450

Tuition Fees: NA

Academic Staff: 40

Campus: Urban, 40 acres

School Colors: NA

Mascot/Nickname: NA

Athletics/Sports Affiliation: NA

Endowment: $51.34

Notable Alumni

Bishop Charles E. Blake: presiding bishop of Church of God in Christ.

Pastor Claudette Anderson Copeland: pastor & cofounder of New Creation Fellowship in San Antonio, Texas.

David M. Copeland: senior pastor of New Creation Fellowship in San Antonio, Texas.

Rev. Connie Jackson: founder & CEO of J Trinity Communications/On the edge ministries, Houston, Texas.

Rev. Candace M. Lewis: New Church Strategist with path 1 New Church at the General Board of Disciples in Nashville, Tennessee.

Dr. Pamela Lightsey: ordained elder of the Northern Illinois Conference of the United Methodist Church.

Dr. Charles R. Stith: director of African American Presidential Archives at Boston University.

Bishop James B. Walker: presiding Prelate of the 9th Episcopal CME District.

Rev. William D. Watley: senior pastor of St Phillip MEC in Atlanta. Georgia.

Dr. R. L. White Jr.: pastor of Mount Ephraim Baptist Church, Atlanta, Georgia.

J. F. Drake State Technical College

History

J.F. Drake State Technical College is a community college in Huntsville, AL. As of the Fall of 2010 semester, Drake State hasan enrollment of 1,258 students. The college was founded in 1961 as the Huntsville State Vocational Technical College. In 1966, the school was renamed as J. F. Drake Technical Trade School in honor of J. F. Drake, a long-serving president of Alabama A&M University. After desegregating in 1967, the school took the name of J. F. Drake Technical College in 1973. In 2013, the college was again renamed after long awaited state approval. The college is now officially known as J. F. Drake State Technical College. This change was petitioned for after the institution earned membership in the SACS in July 2012.

Relevant Information

Established: 1961

Type: Public, HBCU

Location: 3421 Meridian St. N, Huntsville, AL 35811

Phone: 256-539-8161

Religious Affiliation: NA

Student Enrollment: 1,258

Tuition Fees: In-state and out-of-state $19,750

Academic Staff: 103

Campus: Urban, 32 acres

School Colors: Blue and white

Mascot/Nickname: NA

Athletics/Sports Affiliations: NJCAA

Endowment: $39.84 million

Notable Alumni

NA

JACKSON STATE UNIVERSITY

History

Jackson State University (Jackson State or JSU) is a historically black university in Jackson, MS. Founded in 1877 in Natchez, MS, by the American Baptist Home Mission Society of New York, the society moved the school to Jackson in 1882, renaming it as Jackson College, and developed its present campus in 1902. It became a state-supported public institution in 1940. It is a member-school of the Thurgood Marshall College Fund and holds an important place in the history of US civil rights. JSU was started as Natchez Seminary, private school, under the auspices of the American Baptist Home Mission Society. It operated 63 years as a private church school. In 1883, the society moved the school Jackson to the site where Millsaps College now stands. In 1944, the Mississippi Negro Training School was renamed as Jackson College for Negro Teachers. In the 1960s, the entire curriculum was reorganized, and in 1974, Jackson State was designated as JSU.

Relevant Information

Established: 1877

Type: Public, HBCU

Location: 1400 John R. Lynch St., Jackson, MS 39217

Phone: 601-979-2121

Religious Affiliation: American Baptist Home Mission Society

Student Enrollment: 8,887

Tuition Fees: $13,946

Academic Staff: 450

Campus: Urban, 245 acres

School Colors: Navy blue and white

Mascot/Nickname: Tigers

Athletics/Sports Affiliation: NCAA Div. I, SAC, SWAC

Endowment: $12 million

Notable Alumni

Rod Paige: secretary of education during President George W. Bush's administration.

Vivian Brown: Weather Channel meteorologist.

Demarco Morgan: news anchor for WNBC in New York City.

Percy Greene: founded the *Jackson Advocate* newspaper.

Willie Norwood: American gospel singer.

Tonea Stewart: actress and educator.

Cassandra Wilson: jazz vocalist and musician.

Emmett C. Burns: member of Maryland House of Delegates.

Robert G. Clark: first African American elected to the Mississippi State Legislature since Reconstruction Era.

Malcolm D. Jackson: CIO at Environmental Protection Agency under President Barack Obama's administration.

Carlton W. Reeves: judge of the US District Court of Mississippi.

Bennie Thompson: member of the US House of Representatives.

Shasta Averyhardt: female LPGA golfer, first African American to qualify for LPGA tour since 2001.

Lem Barney: NFL Hall of Fame cornerback with the Detroit Lions.

Marcus Benard: currently NFL linebacker.

Dennis "Oil Can" Boyd: former Major League Baseball player.

Corey Bradford: former NFL wide receiver.

Robert Brazile: former seven-time NFL Pro Bowl linebacker with the Houston Oilers.

Wes Chamberlain: former Major League outfielder.

Dave Clark: former Major League outfielder.

Eddie Payton: NFL kick returner.

Walton Payton: NFL Hall of Fame running back for the Chicago Bears.

Archie Cooley: former head football coach at Mississippi Valley State, University of Arkansas, NSU, and Paul Quinn College.

Leslie Duncan: former four-time Pro Bowl cornerback with the San Diego Charges and Washington Red Skins.

Marvin Freeman: former Major League pitcher.

Cletis Gordon: former NFL defensive back.

Claudis James: former NFL player.

Jaymar Johnson: current NFL wide receiver.

Tray Johnson: current NBA Development League player.

Ed Manning: drafted by the Baltimore Bullets of the NBA draft and father of Danny Manning.

Audie Norris: former NBA power forward and superstar for Winterthur FC Barcelona in the late 1980s.

Purvis Short: former NBA small forward for Golden State Warriors.

Jackie Slater: NFL Hall of Fame offensive tackle with the Los Angeles/ St. Louis Rams.

JARVIS CHRISTIAN COLLEGE

History

Jarvis Christian College is an independent, four-year, private, historically black college—affiliated with the Christian Church—that offers associate and bachelor's degrees. It is located in unincorporated Wood County, TX, near Hawkins. Ida Van Zandt Jarvis, who with her husband, deeded 456 acres to the Christian Women's Board of Missions to "keep up and maintain a school for the elevation and education of the Negro race." In 1939, the college was granted its charter by the state of Texas, and in 1950, Jarvis Christian was included by the SACS on its Approved list of Colleges and Universities for Negro Youth, the only regional accreditation available at that time for black colleges in the South.

Relevant Information

Established: 1912

Type: Private, HBCU

Location: US 60, PO Box 1470, Hawking, TX 70765

Phone: 903-730-4890

Religious Affiliation: Christian Church (Disciples of Christ) Student

Enrollment: 546

Tuition Fees: In-state and out-of-state $13,374

Academic Staff: 50

Campus: Rural, 243 acres

School Colors: Royal blue and light gold

Mascot/Nickname: Bulldogs

Athletics/Sports Affiliation: NAIA Div. I, RRAC

Endowment: Assets, $29.03 million

Notable Alumni

Charles A. Berry: eighth president of Jarvis Christian College.

Lorene B. Holmes: educator, author, and professor.

James O. Perpener Jr.: fifth president of Jarvis Christian College.

Homer L. Brown: established Fouke Hawkins School Reunion Scholarship Fund at Jarvis Christian College.

JOHNSON C. SMITH UNIVERSITY

History

JCSU is a private, historically black, coed, four-year research university of higher learning located in Charlotte, NC. It is affiliated with the Presbyterian Church, USA. JCSU offers an assortment of academic programs aimed at ensuring that its graduates are prepared for success in the workforce. From 1921 to 1922, Jane Berry Smith donated funds to build a theological dormitory, a science hall, a teachers' cottage, and a memorial gate. She also provided an endowment for the institution in memory of her late husband, Johnson C. Smith. Until her death, she donated funds for five more buildings and a campus church. In recognition of these generous benefactions, the board of trustees voted to change the name of the institution, in remembrance of her late husband, to JCSU. The charter of the school, accordingly, was amended on March 1, 1923 by the legislature of the state of North Carolina.

Relevant Information

Established: 1867

Type: Private, HBCU

Location: 100 Beatties Ford Rd., Charlotte, NC 28216

Phone: 704-378-1000

Religious Affiliation: Presbyterian Church, USA

Student Enrollment: 1,669

Tuition Fees: In-state and out-of-state $15,466

Academic Staff: 159

Campus: Urban, 105 acres

School Colors: Navy blue and gold

Mascot/Nickname: Bulls

Athletics/Sports Affiliation: NCAA Div. II, ClAA

Endowment: $51.1 million

Notable Alumni

John H. Adams: pastor at Seattle's First AMA Episcopal Church and civil rights leader.

Frederick C. Branch: first African American officer in US Marine Corps.

Eva M. Clayton: first African American elected to the House of Representatives in North Carolina.

Gregory Clifton: NFL player with Washington Red Skins and Carolina Panthers.

Dorothy Counts: one of the first blacks admitted to Harding School in the United States.

Grover Covington: Canadian Football League defensive end for the Hamilton Tiger Cats.

Charlie S. Dannelly: Democratic member of North Carolina General Assembly.

De'Audra Dix: first all-American team and played for Montreal Allouettes in the Canadian Football League.

Edward R. Dudley: first African American to hold rank of ambassador of the United States.

Richard Erwin: first black federal judge in North Carolina.

Ferdinand K. Rawoo: Ghanaian minister of religion, playwright, and educator.

Leford Green: Div. II Collegiate indoor and outdoor Region and National Track Athlete of the year.

Chet Grimsley: first Euro-American to garner accolades as All-CIAA and All-American at JCSU.

Larry D. Hall: American politician from Durham. NC.

Henry Hill: first African American to become president of American Chemical Society.

Cheris F. Hodges: author of African American romance novels.

Josephus Cox: computer engineer, first to obtain this degree from an HBCU.

Earl Manigault: a Rucker Park legend.

Albert Manley: president of Spelman College.

Vincent Matthews: winner of two gold medals at the 1968 Summer Olympics.

Eddie McGirt: a ClAA football legend.

Mildred M. Bateman: first African American woman to be named to high-ranking officer in West Virginia state government.

Fred "Curly" Neal: former member of the Harlem Globetrotters.

Pettis Norman: NFL tight end with the Dallas Cowboys and San Diego Charges.

Obie Patterson: former member of the Maryland House of Delegates.

Don Pullen: jazz pianist and organist.

Sandra L. Townes: district judge of US District Court, NY.

Skeets Tolbert: jazz clarinetist.

Avon Williams: Tennessee state senator.

Robert F. Williams: civil rights leader, author, and president of Monroe, NC, NAACP.

Shermaine Williams: Jamaican track and field sprinter.

Iren G. Wyatt: educator and first black girl scout in North Carolina.

Dorothy C. Yancey: educator and first woman president of Johnson C. Smith University (JCSU) and Shaw University.

John W. Rice: Presbyterian minister, college administrator, and father of former US Secretary of State Condoleezza Rice.

Zilner Randolph: jazz trumpeter.

James "Twiggy" Sanders: Harlem Globetrotters's player.

Gary Siplin: politician and member of Florida Senate.

Marvin Scott: Republican candidate for US Senate from Indiana.

Richard L. Spencer: Grammy Award winner, composer noting his R&B song of the year "Color Him Father."

Clarence F. Stephens: ninth African American to receive a PhD in Mathematics.

Johnny Taylor: pitcher, played in professional pre-league and Negro league from 1903 to 1925.

KENTUCKY STATE UNIVERSITY

History

Kentucky State University (KSU or KYSU to differentiate from Kansas State University) is a four-year, liberal arts institution located in Frankfort, KY, the Commonwealth's capital. The university is a historically black university and the second state-supported, postsecondary institution in Kentucky. It is an 1890 land-grant university that serves the citizens of Kentucky through its cooperative extension program. Half of the student body is currently African American. The school is accredited by the Commission on Colleges of the SACS and is a member-school of the Thurgood Marshall College Fund. The school was chartered in 1887 and opened in 1887 as the State Normal School for Colored Persons. The school became a land-grant institution in 1890. The name of the school was changed to the Kentucky State College for Negroes in 1938.The college became a full-fledged university in 1972. In 1973, KSU offered its first graduate programs.

Relevant Information

Established: 1886

Type: Public, HBCU

Location: 111, Frankfort, KY 40601

Phone: 502-597-6000

Religious Affiliation: NA

Student Enrollment: 2,341

Tuition Fees: In-state $6,858; out-of-state $16,458

Academic Staff: NA

Campus: Rural, 511 acres

School Colors: Green and gold

Mascot/Nickname: Thorobreds and Thorobrettes

Athletics/Sports Affiliations: SIAC, NCAA Div. II

Endowment: $10,581,408

Notable Alumni

Paul W.L. Jones: educator, historian, and athlete; known as the "Father of Athletics" at Kentucky State.

James L. McCullin: Tuskegee Airmen officer.

Ersa H. Poston: first African American to head US Civil Service Commission.

Whitney M. Young: former civil rights leader and executive director of National Urban League.

H. C. Russell: ensign in the US Coast Guard and executive with Coca Cola.

Winnie A. Scott: educator who helped to establish a hospital for African Americans in Frankfort, KY.

Frank Simpson: educator and high school principal for 21 years.

Moneta Sleet: photographer for *Ebony* and Pulitzer Prize winner.

Effie W. Smith: educator and poet.

John Merritt: former head football coach at Jackson State University (JSU) and Tennessee State University.

Davey Whitney: former head basketball coach at TSU and NCB basketball

Hall of Fame.

Walter D. Bean: teacher, principal, and supervisor with Indianapolis Public Schools.

Anthony Beatty: became first African American chief in Lexington, KY.

James T. Beaumont: elected as the first African American councilman in La Grange, KY.

Tuska Twyman: former mayor of Glasgow, KY and first black mayor.

Harrison B. Wilson: second president of Norfolk State College.

Marsha Harpool: first African American mayor of Blountstown, FL.

Yingluck Shinawatra: twenty-eighth and first female prime minister of Thailand.

Margaret E. S. Barnes: editor and trustee at Wilberforce University.

Midnight Star: musical group formed in 1976.

Michael Bernard: basketball player, played in NBA Cincinnati Royals.

Henry E. Cheaney: educator and nationally recognized expert on history of African Americans in Kentucky.

Anna M. Clarke: first African American woman officer of an all-white Women's Army Corps of World War II.

Tom Colbert: first African American Oklahoma Supreme Court Justice.

Travis Grant: college basketball star at KSU and played on NAIA championship teams.

Rod Hill: former professional NFL and CFL football player.

Cletidus Hunt: former professional football player, who played six sessions in the NFL.

Sam Sibert: former college basketball standout, played in NBA Cincinnati Royals.

Elmore Smith: NBA and college basketball player, NAIA, and NCAA.

Herb Trawick: first black to play in CFL and was inducted in Canadian Football Hall of Fame.

Joseph Kendall: former All-American quarterback, inducted into the

College Football Hall of Fame.

Jayjay Helterbrand: Filipino player of the Barangay Ginebra Kings in the Philippine Basketball Association.

Ezzret Anderson: one of the first African Americans to play football with the Los Angeles Dons.

KNOXVILLE COLLEGE

History

Knoxville College is a historically black, liberal arts college in Knoxville, TN. Founded in 1875 by the United Presbyterian Church of North America, the school has an enrollment of approximately 100 students and offers a Bachelor of Science degree in liberal arts studies and an associate arts degree. Knoxville College is a UNCF member-school. It is rooted in a mission school established in Knoxville in 1864 to educate the city's blacks and freed slaves. In 1877, the school was designated as a college by the state. In 1890, the state designated the school as the recipient of Morrill Act funds for blacks with which the school established mechanical and agricultural departments. Due to dire financial problems, the SACS withdrew the college's accreditation. The school's alumni association embarked on an aggressive fund-raising campaign, and the school has gradually re-established itself.

Relevant Information

Established: 1875

Type: Private, HBCU

Location: 901 Knoxville College Dr., Knoxville, TN 37921

129

Phone: 865-524-6525

Religious Affiliation: Presbyterian Church (USA)

Student Enrollment: 100

Tuition Fees: $11,528

Academic Staff: 35

Campus: Urban, 39 acres

School Colors: Garnet and blue

Mascot/Nickname: Bulldogs

Athletics/Sports Affiliation: NA

Endowment: $1 million

Notable Alumni

George E. Curry: editor-in-chief of National Newspaper Publishers Association and chairman of board of trustees at Knoxville College.

Michael E. Dyson: professor of sociology at Georgetown University, author, media commentator, and radio show host.

C. Virginia Fields: social worker and former borough president of Manhattan, NY.

Johnny Ford: mayor of Tuskegee, AL.

Jake Gaither: legendary Florida **A&M** University football coach who won more than 85 percent of his games over a 24-year period.

Grady Jackson: former NFL defensive tackle.

Vernon Jarrett: first African American columnist for the *Chicago Tribune* and former president of the NABJ.

Ken Johnson: former NFL defensive end.

Lyman T. Johnson: educator and influential leader of racial desegregation in the state of Kentucky during the 1940s.

Edith I. Jones: first female president of the National Medical Association.

Barbara Rogers: former anchor of KPIX TV in San Francisco.

Ralph Wiley: noted author and sports columnist for the *Oakland Tribune* and *Sports Illustrated.*

Palmer Williams Jr.: actor star of Tyler Perry's *House of Payne.*

LANE COLLEGE

History

L ane College is a four-year, historically black college—associated with the CME Church—located in Jackson, TN, just northeast of the downtown area. Lane College was founded in 1882 by the CME Church in America as the "CME High School." Planning for the school had begun in 1878, but the school's establishment was delayed by a yellow fever epidemic in the region in 1878. Its primary purpose was to provide education for newly freed slaves, and the original curriculum forced on the preparation of "teachers and preachers." Its academic areas include business science, liberal studies, education, and natural and physical sciences.

Relevant Information

Established: 1882

Type: Private, HBCU

Location: 545 Lane Ave., Jackson, TN 38301

Phone: 731-426-7500

Religious Affiliation: CME Church

Student Enrollment: 2,000

Tuition Fees: $8,560

Academic Staff: NA

Campus: Urban, 25 *acres*

School Colors: Cardinal and royal blue

Mascot/Nickname: Dragons

Athletics/Sports Affiliation: NCAA Div. II, SIAC

Endowment: $4,291,771

Notable Alumni

Timothy T. Jackson: quarterback of the season.

Steve Collins: exemplary linebacker.

Donald L. Hollowell: civil rights lawyer, first African American to be named regional director of US Equal Employment Opportunity Commission.

Jacoby Jones: current professional football player.

Fred Lane: former professional football player.

Jason Brookins: former professional football player.

LAWSON STATE COMMUNITY COLLEGE, BESSEMER CAMPUS

History

Lawson State Community College (Lawson State) is a community college located in Birmingham and Bessemer, AL. It is one of Alabama's oldest state-supported community colleges that opened its doors in 1949. The technical division was established in 1947. This established Wenonah State Technical Institute in 1949. The academic studies began as Lawson State Junior College. The college was opened in 1965 and was named after its first president, T. A. Lawson. In 1973, Wenonah State and Lawson State merged and became one institution known as the LawsonWenonah State Junior College and Technical Institute, shortly thereafter becoming Lawson State Community College.

Relevant Information

Established: 1949

Type: Public, HBCU

Location: 3060 Wilson RD, SW, Birmingham, AL 35221

Phone: 205-925-2515

Religious Affiliation: NA

Student Enrollment: 6,042

Tuition Fees: In-state $4,170; out-of-state $7,290

Academic Staff: NA

Campus: Urban, 50 and 34 acres

School Colors: Yellow and navy blue

Mascot/Nickname: Cougars

Athletics/Sports Affiliation: NJCAA

Endowment: NA

Notable Alumni

Paul Morphy: chess prodigy.

LANGSTON UNIVERSITY

History

Langston University is an institution of higher learning located in Langston, OK. It is the only historically black college in the state and the westernmost historically black college in the United States. Though located in a rural setting just ten miles east of Guthrie, Langston also serves as an urban mission with University Centers in both Tulsa and Oklahoma City. The university is a member-school of the Thurgood Marshall College Fund. The school was founded in 1897 and was known as the Oklahoma Colored Agricultural and Normal University. Langston University was created as a result of the second Morrill Act in 1890. The law required states with land-grant colleges (such as Oklahoma State University, then Oklahoma A&M) to either admit African Americans or provide an alternative school for them to attend as a condition of receiving federal funds. Langston University is named after John M. Langston, a civil rights pioneer, first African American member of Congress from Virginia.

Relevant Information

Established: 1897

Type: Public, HBCU

Location: 701 Sammy Davis Junior Dr., Langston, OK 73050

Phone: 405-466-2231

Religious Affiliation: NA

Student Enrollment: 3,922

Tuition Fees: In-state $4,255; out-of-state $10,741

Academic Staff: NA

Campus: Rural, 40 acres

School Colors: Navy blue and orange

Mascot/Nickname: Lions

Athletics/Sports Affiliation: NAIA, RRAC

Endowment: $35,241,841

Notable Alumni

Bessie Coleman: first African American woman pilot to obtain an International Pilot's license.

James Rosser: president of California State University for almost three decades.

Matthew Hatchette: wide receiver for the Minnesota Vikings, New York Jets, Oakland Raiders, and Jacksonville Jaguars.

Robert DoQui: actor.

Maurice "Mo" Bassett: former NFL fullback for Cleveland's Brown.

Ada L. S. Fisher: stood at the forefront of the fight to integrate white schools in the South.

William H. Hale: past president of Langston University and Alpha Phi Alpha Fraternity.

The Delta Rhythm Boys: vocal group inducted into the Vocal Group Hall of Fame.

Nathan Hare: founding publisher of *The Black Scholar* and first person hired to coordinate a black studies program in the United States.

Marques Haynes: basketball and football star before going on to captain the Harlem Globetrotters.

Thomas "Hollywood" Henderson: Pro-Bowl linebacker for the Dallas Cowboys.

Ernest L. Holloway: past president of Langston University.

Clara Luper: civil rights leader best known for her leadership in the Oklahoma City Sit-in Movement.

Nancy Riley: former member of the Oklahoma senate.

Henry Ponder: past president of Fisk University, Talladega College, Benedict College, and NAFEO.

Mike Shelton: member of Oklahoma House of Representatives.

Norma Tucker: past president of Merritt College.

William Hytche: past president of UMES.

Col. Michael C. Thompson: member of Oklahoma Highway Patrol with rank of OHP major.

LeMoyne-Owen College

History

LeMoyne-Owen College is a fully accredited, four-year, private,historically black college located in Memphis, TN, affiliated with the United Church of Christ. It resulted from the 1968 merger of institutions who traced their historically black roots to some of the earliest endeavors to educate former slaves in the 1860s. LeMoyne-Owen College was formed through the merger of LeMoyne College and Owen College, both historically black, church-affiliated colleges. LeMoyne Normal and Commercial School traces its history to 1862 when the AMA opened an elementary school for freedmen and escaped slaves. Owen College traces its history as a junior college to 1947 when the Tennessee Baptist Missionary and Educational Convention bought property on Vance Avenue to open the school in 1954.

Relevant Information

Established: 1968

Type: Private, HBCU

Location: 807 Walker Ave., Memphis, TN 38126

Phone: 901-435-1500

Religious Affiliation: United Church of Christ

Student Enrollment: 600

Tuition Fees: $10,538

Academic Staff: NA

Campus: Urban, 25 acres

School Colors: Gold and purple

Mascot/Nickname: Magicians

Athletics/Sports Affiliation: NCAA Div. Ill, NAIA, and SIAC

Endowment: NA

Notable Alumni

Lloyd Barbee: Wisconsin legislator and civil rights activist.

Marion Barry: former mayor of Washington, D.C. and currently
Washington, D.C. city council member.

W. Herenton: former mayor of Memphis, TN.

Benjamin Hooks: former executive director of NAACP.

Myron Lowery: former mayor of Memphis, TN.

LEWIS COLLEGE OF BUSINESS

History

L ewis College of Business is an unaccredited institution of higher education in Detroit, MI. It is the first historically black college in Michigan. It was founded at the beginning of the Great Depression in 1928 by Violet T. Lewis, an African American female. Lewis College of Business has lost its accreditation, putting the future of the Detroit institution on shaky ground. The decision by the Higher Learning Commission means the college's 250 students will no longer have access to federal financial aid, and other institutions may not recognize Lewis's transfer credits. In 2007, the commission determined that the college no longer met their criteria for accreditation as the HCL withdrew Lewis College of Business's accreditation.

Relevant Information

Established: 1928

Type: Private, HBCU

Location: 17370 Meyers Rd., Detroit, MI 48235

Phone: 313-862-6300

Religious Affiliation: NA

Student Enrollment: 300

Tuition Fees: In-state and out-of-state $7,584

Academic Staff: NA

Campus: Urban, acreage: NA

School Colors: NA

Mascot/Nickname: NA

Athletics/Sports Affiliation: NA

Endowment: NA

Notable Alumni

NA

LINCOLN UNIVERSITY (PENNSYLVANIA)

History

L incoln University of Pennsylvania is the US first degree-granting, historically black university. Founded as a private university since 1972, it is a public institution, located near the town of Oxford in southern Chester County, PA. Lincoln University provides undergraduate degrees to approximately 2,500 students. It was noted that Lincoln University was the first institution in the world to provide higher education in the field of arts and sciences for youth of African descent. The school is a member-school of the Thurgood Marshall College Fund. The university has an impressive list of notable alumni which include US Supreme Court Justice, Thurgood Marshall; Harlem Renaissance poet, Langston Hughes; musical legend, Cab Calloway; the first president of Nigeria, Nnamdi Azikiwe; the first president of Ghana, Kwame Nkrumah; song artist and activist, Gil Scott-Heron; and Tony Award-winning actor, Roscoe L. Browne.

Relevant Information

Established: 1854

Type: State-related, public

Location: 1570 Baltimore Pike, Lincoln University, PA 19352

143

Phone: 610-832-8300

Religious Affiliation: NA

Student Enrollment: 2,649

Tuition Fees: In-state $17,106; out-of-state $29,856

Academic Staff: NA

Campus: Rural, 422 acres

School Colors: Blue and orange

Mascot/Nickname: Lion

Athletics/Sports Affiliation: NCAA Div. II, CIAA and ECAC

Endowment: $23 million

Notable Alumni

Horace M. Bond: past president of Lincoln University and first African American president.

Maria L. Bustill: teacher and mother of Paul Robeson.

Oscar Brown Jr.: singer, actor, and playwright.

William D. Robeson: minister and father of Paul Robeson.

Alexander Dames: became the second African American physician in Florida.

Walter Alexander: first African American to serve in New Jersey Legislature.

Harry W. Bass: first African American elected to the Pennsylvania General Assembly.

A. Birch Jr.: first African American to serve as chief justice of Tennessee Supreme Court.

Donald Bogle: film historian, author, and educator.

Robert Garter: general counsel of NAACP and US District Judge.

Frank Coleman: educator.

Lillian E. Fishburne: first African American woman promoted to rank of rear admiral in US Navy.

Christian Reetwood: served in Union Army during the American Civil War and earned the Medal of Honor.

Archibald H. Grimke: lawyer, journalist public speaker, and member of Niagara Movement.

Joseph W. Holley: founder of Albany State University.

Roderick L. Ireland: first African American associate justice of Massachusetts Supreme Court.

Montford Irvin: New York Baseball Giants player, inducted into Baseball Hall of Fame.

Pee Wee Kirkland: former street baseball player from New York City at Rock Park.

Robert W. Johnson: coach of tennis players Althea Gibson and Arthur Ashe.

Melvin B. Tolson: architect of debate team portrayed in the film *The Great Debaters*.

Hildrus A. Poindexter: internationally known authority on tropical diseases.

Jacqueline Allen: judge for the court of Common Pleas.

Eric C. Webb: author, poet, and editor-in-chief of *Souls of People*.

LINCOLN UNIVERSITY (MISSOURI)

History

Lincoln University of Missouri, a historically black college, is located in Jefferson City, MO. In 2007, Lincoln University was ranked number three for economic diversity and number nine for most international students among master's level universities in the Midwest. The university is a member-school of the Thurgood Marshall College Fund. The school was founded as Lincoln Institute in 1866 by members of the 62nd and 65th US Colored Infantry. They intended to provide education to African Americans through the combining of academics and labor in the industrial school model characteristic of Booker T. Washington's Institute. Under the Morrill Act of 1890, Missouri designated the school as a land-grant university, emphasizing agriculture, mechanics, and teaching. In 1921, the college had expanded to offer graduate programs and was officially designated a university by the State of Missouri and changed its name to Lincoln University of Missouri.

Relevant Information

Established: 1866

Type: Public, HBCU

Location: 820 Chestnut St., Jefferson City, MO 65101

Phone: 573-681-5000

Religious Affiliation: NA

Student Enrollment: 3,156

Tuition Fees: In-state $6,478; out-of-state $11,965

Academic Staff: NA

Campus: Urban, 167 acres

School Colors: Navy blue and white

Mascot/Nickname: Blue Tigers

Athletics/Sports Affiliation: NCAA Div. II, MIAA

Endowment: NA

Notable Alumni

Rita H. Days: member of both houses of the Missouri State Legislature.

Mervyn M. Dymally: member of the US House of Representatives from California.

Lloyd L. Gaines: disappeared mysteriously after fighting for the right to equal education.

George Howard Jr.: first African American federal judge in Arkansas.

Leo Lewis: member of the Canadian Football Hall of Fame.

Carey Means: voice actor best known for playing Frylock in *Aqua Teen Hunger Force.*

Zeke Moore: former NFL defensive back.

Oliver Lake: jazz musician.

Julius Hemphill: jazz musician.

Lemar Parrish: former eight-time pro NFL defensive back.

Wendell O. Pruitt: US Army captain fighter with the famed 332nd Fighter Group.

Joe Torry: actor and comedian.

Ronald Townson: American vocalist and a member of the 5th Dimension vocal group.

Maida Coleman: State Minority leader in Missouri.

Blain Luetkemeyer: US Congressman.

William T. Vernon: minister and bishop of the AME Church.

LIVINGSTONE COLLEGE

History

Livingstone College is a private, historically black, four-year college in Salisbury, NC. It is affiliated with the AME Zion Church. Livingstone College is accredited by the Commission on Colleges of the SACS to award the Bachelor of Arts, Bachelor of Science, Bachelor of Fine Arts, and Bachelor of Social Work degrees. Livingstone College along with Hood Theological Seminary began as Zion Wesley Institute in Concord, NC, in 1879. The school was closed in Concord and reopened in 1882, a few miles north in Salisbury. Zion Wesley Institute was originally founded by the AME Zion Church. The institute changed its name to Livingstone College in 1887 to honor African Missionary David Livingstone. That same year, the school granted its first degree. It has sewn structures that are listed on the National Register of Historic Places.

Relevant Information

Established: 1879

Type: Private, HBCU

Location: 701 West Monroe St., Salisbury, NC 28144

Phone: 800-835-3435

Religious Affiliation: AME Zion Church

Student Enrollment: 1,200

Tuition Fees: $15,708

Academic Staff: 80

Campus: Urban, 272 acres

School Colors: Columbia blue and black

Mascot/Nickname: Blue Bear

Athletics/Sports Affiliation: NCAA Div. II, CIAA

Endowment: $1,534,413

Notable Alumni

James E. K. Aggrey: influential Pan-African thinker, educator, and Christian preacher.

George L. Blackwell: theologian and author.

Ben Coates: former tight end for New England Patriots and Baltimore Ravens.

Elizabeth D. Koontz: first black president of the NEA and head of Women's Bureau of US Department of Labor.

Vergel L. Lattimore: brigadier general of Air National Guard.

Rev. John Kinard: community activist and first director of the Anacostia (DC) Neigborhood Community Museum.

Wilmont Perry: former NFL running back for the New Orleans Saints.

UNIVERSITY OF MARYLAND EASTERN SHORE

History

The UMES—located in Princess Ann, MD—is a part of the University System of Maryland and is a historically black, land-grant university. The school was founded in 1886 through the offices of the Delaware Conference Academy. Later, UMES came to be called Industrial Branch of Morgan State College and Princess Anne Academy. The University of Maryland, College Park, did not admit African Americans and sought to provide a land- grant school for African Americans. In 1919, the State of Maryland assumed control and changed its name to Eastern Shore Branch of the Maryland Agricultural College. In 1948, the name was again changed to Maryland State College. In 1970, the university obtained its current name of the UMES.

Relevant Information

Established: 1886

Type: Public, HBCU

Location: 11868 Academic Oval, Princess Ann, MD 21853

Phone: 410-651-2200

Religious Affiliation: NA

Student Enrollment: 4,509

Tuition Fees: $16,787 per year

Academic Staff: 310

Campus: Rural, 1,100 acres

Schools: Gray and maroon

Mascot/Nickname: Hawks

Athletics/Sports Affiliation: NCAA Div. I, MEAC

Endowment: $24,632,367

Notable Alumni

Emerson Boozer: former NFL player.

Roger Brown: former NFL player.

Earl Christy: former NFL player.

Clarence Clemons: saxophonist with Bruce Springsteen and the E Street Band.

James Duncan: former NFL player.

Starletta DuPois: actress.

Carl Hairston: former NFL player.

Merrecia James: track and field distant runner and competed in American Central Caribbean Cross Country Meets.

Charlie Mays: former Olympic long jumper and New Jersey state assemblyman.

Earl Richardson: president of MSU.

Chantelle Ringgold: former volleyball, track and field player, who played in the Lingerie Football League.

Russ Rogers: track standout.

Johnny Sample: former NFL player.

Art Shell: NFL Hall of Fame player and head football coach of the Oakland Raiders.

Ira Smith: former Minor League baseball player, having the highest batting average in Division I.

Charlie Stukes: former NFL player.

Billy Thompson: former NFL player.

Carl Whyte: star track and field athlete, competed on Big Break.

Hoover J. Wright: former head football and track coach at PVAMU.

Billy Thompson: former NFL player.

MEHARRY MEDICAL COLLEGE

History

Meharry Medical College—located in Nashville, TN—is a graduate and professional institution affiliated with the United Methodist Church, whose mission is to educate healthcare professionals and scientists. Founded in 1876 as the Medical Department of Central Tennessee College, it was the first medical school in the South for African Americans. It was charted separately in 1915. It is currently the largest, private, historically black institution in the United States solely dedicated to educating healthcare professionals and scientists. The college was named for a young Scots-Irish immigrant salt trader named Samuel Meharry, who was traveling through the rough terrain of Tennessee when his wagon suddenly slipped off the road and fell into a swamp. Meharry was helped by a family of freedmen. The family of freed slaves gave Meharry food and shelter in the night. The next morning they helped him to recover his wagon. Meharry is reported to have told the former slave family, "I have no money, but when I can, I shall do something for your race." In 1875, Samuel Meharry, together with four of his brothers, donated a total of $15,000 to assist with the establishment of a medical department at Central Tennessee College. The medical department was opened in 1876.

Relevant Information

Established: 1876

Type: Private, HBCU

Location: 1005 Todd Blvd., Nashville, TN 37208

Phone: 615-327-6000

Religious Affiliation: United Methodist Church

Student Enrollment: 700

Tuition Fees: In-state and out-of-state $17,685

Academic Staff: 220

Campus: Urban, acres NA

School Colors: NA

Mascot/Nickname: NA

Athletics/Sports Affiliation: NA

Endowment: $112,455,467

Notable Alumni

E. A. Rankin: chief of orthopedics at Providence Hospital.

Willie Adams Jr.: mayor of Albany, GA.

Billy R. Ballard: first African American board certified oral pathologist.

Hastings K. Banda: president of the Republic of Malawi.

Edward S. Cooper: president of the American Heart Association.

Reginald Coopwood: CEO of the Regional Medical Center at Memphis.

Cleveland Eneas Sr.: senator, Government of the Bahamas.

Sandra Gadson: former president of the National Medical Association.

Robert W. Johnson: tennis instructor for Althea Gibson and Arthur Ashe.

Keith P. Kittelberger: well-known pain medicine anesthesiologist.

Robert Lee: dentist who emigrated to Ghana and offered a dentist practice for nearly five decades.

Audrey F. Manley: deputy surgeon general of the United States.

John E. Maupin: president of Morehouse School of Medicine.

Conrad Murray: personal physician of Michael Jackson.

Leonard Randolph Jr.: acting deputy assistant secretary of defense.

Louis Christopher: dentist and civil rights leader.

Charles V. Roman: president of the National Medical Association.

Walter R. Tucker Jr.: former mayor of Compton, CA.

Matthew Walker Sr.: former professor and chair of the Department of Surgery, Meharry Medical College.

Reuben Warren: associate director for Minority Health, Centers for Disease Control and Prevention.

Charles H. Wright: founder of the Charles H. Wright Museum of African American History.

Jeanne Spurlock: noted psychiatrist and chairman of Department of Psychiatry, Meharry Medical College.

Emily F. Pollard: noted plastic surgeon.

Cart C. Bell: community psychiatrist, international researcher, academician, and author.

MILES COLLEGE

History

Miles College is a historically black college founded in 1898. It is located in Fairfield, AL, 6 miles west of Birmingham. It is a private, liberal arts institution of the CME Church. It is a member of the UNCF. Miles College was organized in 1893 and was founded in 1898 by the Colored Methodist Church. It was chartered as Miles Memorial College in honor of Bishop William H. Miles. In 1941, the name was changed to Miles College. Miles is accredited by the Commission on Colleges of the SACS (for the awarding of baccalaureate degrees), the Alabama State Department of Education, and the Council of Social Work Education. Miles College offers twenty-five bachelor's degrees in divisions of business and accounting, communication, education, humanities, natural sciences and mathematics, social and behavioral sciences. It is one of the sixteen schools in the nation with a Center of Academic Excellence under the Director of National Intelligence.

Relevant Information

Established: 1898

Type: Private, HBCU

Location: 5501 Myron Massey Blvd., Fairfield, AL 35064

Phone: 205-929-1000

Religious Affiliation: CME Church

Student Enrollment: 1,900

Tuition Fees: $10,490

Academic Staff: NA

Campus: Urban, 76 acres

School Colors: Purple and gold

Mascot/Nickname: Golden Bears

Athletics/Sports Affiliation: NCAA Div. I, SIAC

Endowment: $12 million

Notable Alumni

U. W. Clemon: first African American federal judge in the state of Alabama.

Angelena Rice: teacher of high school music and science and mother of former US Secretary of State Condoleezza Rice.

Richard Arrington Jr.: first African American mayor of the city of Birmingham.

Thales McReynolds: former NBA player.

Bennett M. Stewart: former US Representative from Illinois.

Paul A. G. Stewart: fiftieth bishop of CME Church.

Cleopatra Tucker: politician who served in the New Jersey General Assembly.

MISSISSIPPI VALLEY STATE UNIVERSITY

History

Mississippi Valley State University (commonly referred to as MVSU) is a historically black university located in unincorporated Leflore County, MS, in the Mississippi Delta, near Itta Bena. MVSU is a member-school of theThurgood Marshall College Fund. The institution, which opened in 1950, was created by the Mississippi Legislature as Mississippi Vocational College. To attract the support of those who opposed any government action to provide higher education for blacks, those proposing creation of MBC used the term "vocational" to imply that the institution's main purpose would be to train blacks to take on blue-collar jobs.

In 1964, Mississippi Vocational College was renamed as Mississippi Valley State College. In the early 1970s, civil rights leaders continued to protest the inequalities in higher education opportunities offered to whites and blacks in Mississippi. In an effort to defuse some of the criticism, the governor, William Waller, proposed changing the names of three black institutions from "colleges" to "universities." Thus, in 1974, the institution was renamed again as MVSU.

Relevant Information

Established: 1950

Type: Public, HBCU

Location: 14000 Highway 82 West, Itta Bena, MS 38941

Phone: 662-254-9041

Religious Affiliation: NA

Student Enrollment: 2,500

Tuition Fees: In-state $6,036; out-of-state $8,804

Academic Staff: NA

Campus: Rural, 460 acres

School Colors: Forest green and white

Mascot/Nickname: Devils

Athletics/Sports Affiliation: NCAA Div. I, FCS, SWAG

Endowment: $1,687,329

Notable Alumni

Katie Hall: former US Representative from Indiana and former city clerk of Gary, IN.

David L. Jordan: Mississippi state senator since 1993.

Ferr Smith: Mississippi state representative since 1993.

Willie Totten: former head coach of the Delta Devils football team.

Jerry Rice: former NFL wide receiver and Pro Football Hall of Fame member.

Patricia Hoskins: former player with the women's basketball team, the Devilletes.

Ashley Ambrose: former NFL cornerback.

Fred Bohannon: former NFL defensive back.

Vincent Brown: former NFL linebacker and currently college football coach.

Parnell Dickinson: former NFL quarterback.

Ricky Feacher: former NFL wide receiver.

Alphonso Ford: former NBA and Euroleague basketball player.

James Haynes: former NFL linebacker for New Orleans Saints.

Corey Holmes: mayor of Metcalfe, MS and CFL running back.

George Ivory: current head basketball coach at University of Arkansas at Pine Bluff (UAPB), AR.

Deacon Jones: former NFL defensive end and member of Pro Football Hall of Fame.

Melvin Morgan: former NFL defensive back.

Tyrone Timmons: Arena Football wide receiver.

Ted Washington: former NFL linebacker.

MOREHOUSE COLLEGE

History

Morehouse College is a private, all-male, liberal arts, historically black college located in Atlanta, GA. Along with Hampden-Sydney College and Wabash College, Morehouse is one of the three remaining traditional men's liberal arts colleges in the United States. In 1879, the institution moved to its own location and changed its name to Atlanta Baptist Seminary. It later acquired a 4-acre campus in downtown Atlanta. In 1879, the school was renamed Atlanta Baptist College. In 1906, Dr. John Hope became the first African American president of the school. He envisioned an academically rigorous school that would be the antithesis to Booker T. Washington's view of agricultural and trade-focused education for African Americans. In 1913, the college was renamed Morehouse College in honor of Dr. Henry Morehouse, corresponding secretary of the American Baptist Home Mission Society, who had long organized Rockefeller and the Society's support for the college. Morehouse entered into a cooperative agreement with Clark College and Spelman College in 1929 and later expanded the association to form the Atlanta University Center.

Relevant Information

Established: 1867

Type: Private, HBCU, male only

Location: 830 Westview Dr., Southwest, Atlanta, GA 30314

Phone: 404-681-2800

Religious Affiliation: Atlanta Baptist Seminary, Atlanta Baptist College

Student Enrollment: 2,439

Tuition Fees: $22,444

Academic Staff: NA

Campus: Urban, 61 acres

School Colors: White and maroon

Mascot/Nickname: Tigers

Athletics/Sports Affiliation: SIAC, NCAA Div. II

Endowment: $72.9 million

Notable Alumni

Martin Luther King Jr.: activist, humanitarian, and leader of the African American Civil Rights Movement.

Herman Cain: former Republican presidential candidate.

Howard Thurman: theologian.

Spike Lee: filmmaker.

Robert G. Christie: filmmaker.

Samuel L. Jackson: actor.

Gang Star Guru: rapper.

Edwin Moses: Olympic gold medalist.

Lloyd McNeill: jazz flutist, USPS Kwanza Stamp designer.

Walter Massey: former Bank of America chairman.

Maynard Jackson: first African American mayor of Atlanta.

Donn Clendenon: Major League baseball first baseman and 1969 World Services MVP.

Louis W. Sullivan: former US Secretary of Health and Human Services.

David Satcher: former US Surgeon General.

Nima Warfield: school's first Rhodes Scholar.

Christopher Elders: school's second Rhodes Scholar.

Note: Seven other Morehouse graduates have become Fulbright Scholars. Five have become Marshall Scholars. Five have become Luce Scholars, and four have become Watson Scholars.

MOREHOUSE SCHOOL OF MEDICINE

History

Morehouse School of Medicine was founded originally as a part of Morehouse College in 1975 during the tenure of college president Hugh M. Gloster, with Louis W. Sullivan as dean. The School of Medicine at Morehouse College began as a two-year program in basic sciences. The first students were admitted in 1978 and transferred to other medical schools for the clinical years of their training. The school became independent from Morehouse College in 1981. Former US Surgeon General Dr. David Satcher assumed the role of interim president in addition to being the director of the National Center for Primary Care, which is located at the Morehouse School of Medicine. Later, he was named as a full president.

Relevant Information

Established: 1975

Type: Private, medical school

Location: 720 Westview Dr. SW, Atlanta, GA 30310

Phone: 404-752-1500

Religious Affiliation: NA

Student Enrollment: 236

Tuition Fees: In-state and out-of-state $73,522

Academic Staff: 250

Campus size: NA

School Colors: NA

Mascot/Nickname: NA

Athletics/Sports Affiliation: NA

Endowment: $56.4 millions

Notable Alumni

NA

MORGAN STATE UNIVERSITY

History

Morgan State University (MSU) was founded in 1867 as the Centenary Biblical institute, a Methodist Episcopal Seminary, to train young men in ministry. The seminary endowed the Male Free School and Colored Institute through legacy to broaden its mission to educate both men and women. In 1915, Andrew Carnegie gave the school a grant of $50,000 for a central academic building. After a controversy was upheld by the circuit court, recording the school as having been sold to a "negro college," Morgan College was allowed to be constructed at the new site and was later expanded. Morgan remained a private institution until 1939. That year, the State of Maryland purchased the school in response to a state study that determined that Maryland needed to provide more opportunities for its black citizens. Morgan College became MSU. In 1975, Morgan added several doctoral programs and its board of directors petitioned the Maryland Legislature to grant university status.

Relevant Information

Established: 1867

Type: Public, HBCU

Location: 1700 E Cold Spring Ln., Baltimore, MD 21251

Phone: 443-885-3333

Religious Affiliation: Methodist Episcopal

Student Enrollment: 6,591

Tuition Fees: In-state $17,890; out-of-state $27,234

Academic Staff: 437

Campus: Urban, 143 acres

School Colors: Blue and orange

Mascot/Nickname: Bear

Athletics/Sports Affiliation: NCAA Div. I, MEAC

Endowment: $20,980,948

Notable Alumni

Willie Lanier: NFL Football Hall of Fame.

Roosevelt Brown: NFL Football Hall of Fame.

Leroy Kelly: NFL Football Hall of Fame.

Len Ford: NFL Football Hall of Fame.

Earl Graves: publisher, *Black Enterprise* magazine.

William Ward: first commanding officer of the US African Command.

William C. Rhoden: *New York Times'* sports columnist and playwright.

David E. Talbert: entrepreneur.

Zaina Adamu: CNN video journalist.

MORRIS BROWN COLLEGE

History

Morris Brown College (MBC) is a private, coed, liberal arts college located in the Vine City community of Atlanta, GA. It is a historically black college affiliated with the AME Church. Although MBC is not a member of the Atlanta Center Consortium, it is located within the Atlanta University Center (a district designated by the Atlanta City Council). Eight percent of the school's 2,500 students receive financial aid from the federal government, which gave MBC $8 million dollars a year. In 2002, it lost its accreditation and federal funding due to a financial mismanagement scandal during the 1998-2002 school years. In August 2012, MBC filed for Chapter 11 bankruptcy in an attempt to prevent foreclosure and sale of the school at auction. Both the alumni association and the African Episcopal Church have pledged to keep the school from dosing.

Relevant Information

Established: 1881

Type: Private, HBCU

Location: 643 Martin Luther King Dr. SW, Atlanta, GA 30314

Phone: 404-739-1010

Religious Affiliation: AME Church

Student Enrollment: 240

Tuition Fees: In-state and out-of-state $9,769

Academic Staff: NA

Campus: Urban, 21 acres

School Colors: Purple and black

Mascot/Nickname: Wolverines

Athletics/Sports Affiliation: Discontinued

Endowment: Estimated $5 million

Notable Alumni

Eula Adams: executive vice president of First Data Corporation.

George Atkinson: former NFL defensive back for Oakland Raiders.

Thomas Byrd: television, film, and stage actor.

Derrick Boazman: local Atlanta radio talk show host and former Atlanta city councilman.

Ezell Brown: educational entrepreneur and founder of Education Online Services Corporation.

Gloria E. Cain: wife of Herman Cain.

Marilyn Cunningham-Kenoly: chief information officer of Kenoly Emerging Technologies, LLC.

Dante Curry: former NFL linebacker for Carolina Panthers and Detroit Lions.

Albert J. Edmonds: retired lieutenant general of the US Air Force.

Tommy Hart: former NFL defensive end for the San Francisco 49ers.

Alfred Jenkins: former NFL and WFL wide receiver for Atlanta Facons and Birmingham Americans.

Ezra Johnson: former NFL defensive end for the Green Bay Packers and

Indianapolis Colts.

James A. McPherson: Pulitzer prize-winning author.

Billy Nicks: former head football coach of MBC and PVAMU.

Sommore: comedian and member of the *Queens of Comedy.*

Hosea Williams: civil rights activist.

MORRIS COLLEGE

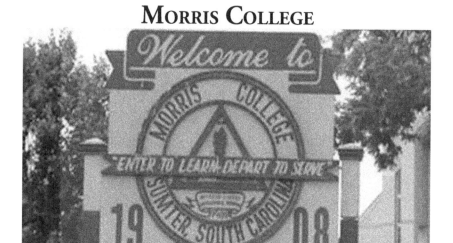

History

Morris College (MC), located in Sumter, SC, is a four-year, coeducational, liberal arts, private, historically black college founded and operated by the Baptist Educational and Missionary Convention of South Carolina. MC was founded in 1908, initially as a grade school, high school, and college. The college is named after Rev. Frank Morris because of his outstanding leadership throughout the African American community of South Carolina. MC awarded its first bachelor's degree in 1915. The college is accredited by the SACS and awards four different types of bachelor's degrees. To effectively accomplish the purpose and philosophy of MC, its academic programs are organized into six academic divisions that oversee their respective departments.

Relevant Information

Established: 1908

Type: Private, HBCU

Location: 100 West College St., Sumter, SC 29150

Phone: 803-778-1620

Religious Affiliation: Baptist Educational and Missionary Convention of

South Carolina

Student Enrollment: 900

Tuition Fees: In-state $10,840; out-of-state $15,606

Academic Staff: 50

Campus: Urban, 40 acres

School Colors: Blue and gold

Mascot/Nickname: Hornets

Athletics/Sports Affiliation: NAIA Div. I

Endowment: NA

Notable Alumni

J. D. Weeks: member of the South Carolina House of Representatives and Chair of Legislative Black Caucus.

Laura Hall: member of Alabama House of Representatives.

Jerry Moore: Freedom Rides participant.

Herman Harris: Freedom Rides participant.

Mae F. Moultrie: Freedom Rides participant.

James T. McCain: civil rights activist, local president of CORE.

Leroy Bowman: legendary Tuskegee Airmen of World War II.

NORFOLK STATE UNIVERSITY

History

NSU is a four-year, state-supported, coed, liberal arts, historically black university located in Norfolk, VA. The institution was founded in 1935 as the Norfolk Unit of Virginia Union University. In 1942, the school became independent of VUU and was named Norfolk Polytechnic College. *Within* two years, the Virginia Legislature made it a part of Virginia State College (now Virginia State University). In 1969, the college divided from Virginia State College and was named Norfolk State College. In 1979, the General Assembly of Virginia granted university status for the school which now has the name of NSU. The university is a member-school of the Thurgood Marshall College Fund and the Virginia High Tech Partnership.

Relevant Information

Established: 1935

Type: Public, HBCU

Location: 700 Park Ave., Norfolk, VA 23504

Phone: 757-823-8600

Religious Affiliation: NA

Student Enrollment: 7,000

Tuition Fees: In-state $6,700; out-of-state $20,343

Academic Staff: 285

Campus: Urban, 134 acres

School Colors: Green and gold

Mascot/Nickname: Spartans

Athletics/Sports affiliation: NCAA Div. I, MEAC

Endowment: $23 million

Notable Alumni

Willard Bailey: former head football coach at Virginia Union University, NSU, and Saint Paul's College.

Gordon Banks: guitarist, producer, writer, and music director.

Al Beard: former ABA player for the New Jersey Americans.

Ron Bolton: former NFL player for the New England Patriots and the Cleveland Browns.

Karen Briggs: violinist. Vincent Brothers:convicted American mass murderer.

Chris Brown: Bahamian track and field sprinter.

Don Carey: NFL defensive back.

Bob Dandridge: former NBA player for the Milwaukee Bucks and the Washington Bullets.

Derek T. Dingle: senior vice president/editor-in-chief of *Black Enterprise* magazine.

Ray Epps: former NBA player for the Golden State Warriors.

Evelyn J. Fields: former director of the Office of the National Oceanic and Atmospheric Administration.

Future Man: percussionist and member of the jazz quartet Béla Fleck and Flecktones.

Willie Gillus: former NFL player for the Green Bay Packers.

Paul Hines: football coach and inspiration for Denzel Washington's character in the film *Remember the Titans*.

Pee Wee Kirkland: NBA draft pick and notable Rucker Park street basketball star.

Ray Jarvis: former NFL player for Atlanta Falcons, Buffalo Bills, Detroit Lions, and New England Patriots.

Lee Johnson: former NBA player for Detroit Pistons.

Leroy Jones: former NFL player for the San Diego Chargers.

Nathan McCall: former reporter for the *Virginian Pilot-Ledger Star, The Atlanta Journal-Constitution,* and the *Washington Post.*

Jon McKinney: former NBA player for the Boston Celtics.

Yvonne B. Miller: Democratic state senator of the Commonwealth of Virginia.

Kyle O'Quinn: NBA player for the Orlando Magic.

David Pope: former NBA player for the Utah Jazz, Kansas City Kings, and the Seattle SuperSonics.

Ken Reaves: former NFL player for the Atlanta Falcons, New Orleans Saints, and St. Louis Cardinals.

Tim Reid: comedian, actor, and director.

Randall Robinson: lawyer, author, and activist, who is noted as the founder of TransAfrica.

James E. Roe: former NFL player for Baltimore Ravens and Arena Football League player for the San Jose SaberCats.

Chandra Sturrup: Bahamian tract sprinter.

Shawn Z. Tarrant: member *of* Maryland House of Delegates.

Andrew Warren: former US diplomat to Algeria.

Susan Wigenton: federal judge, US District Court.

NORTH CAROLINA A&T
STATE UNIVERSITY

History

North Carolina A&T State University (NC A&T or A&T) is a land-grant university located in Greensboro, NC. It is the largest publicly funded, historically black college (HBCU) in the state of North Carolina. NC A&T is a constituent institution of the University System of North Carolina. It is accredited by the SACS and classified as a research university with high research activity by the Carnegie Classification of Institutions of Higher Education. Founded in 1891 and known then as the Agricultural and Mechanical College for the Colored Race, NC A&T is one of the nation's leading producers of African American engineers with bachelor's, master's, and doctorate degrees. NASA is one of the major partners of the School of Engineering. It is also the nation's top producer of minorities with degrees in science, engineering, minority-certified public accountants, landscape architects, and veterinarians. NC A&T is a member-school of the Thurgood Marshall College Fund.

Relevant Information

Established: 1891

Type: Public, HBCU, land-grant

Location: 1601 East Market St., Greensboro, NC 27411

Phone: 336-125-6006

Religious Affiliation: NA

Student Enrollment: 10,383

Tuition Fees: In-state $5,199; out-of-state $15,797

Academic Staff: NA

Campus: Urban, 200 acres

School Colors: Blue and gold

Mascot/Nickname: Aggies

Athletics/Sports Affiliation: NCAA Div. I, MEAC

Endowment: $29,473,552

Notable Alumni

Tevester Anderson: Jackson State University men's basketball coach.

George Small: former NFL player and currently Florida A&M defensive line coach.

Al Attles: former NBA player and currently vice president of Golden State Warriors.

Warren Ballentine: attorney and syndicated radio talk show host.

Elvin Bethea: former NFL defensive lineman for the Houston Oilers and member of Pro Football Hall of Fame.

Dwaine Board: NFL player and currently defensive line coach.

Walter Carter: civil rights activist.

Lou Donaldson: jazz musician.

Joe Dudley: founder of Dudley Products Inc.

Curtis Deloatch: former NFL defensive back.

Hugh Evans: former NBA referee.

James A. Hefner: renowned economist and university president.

Taraji P. Henson: actress.

Maurice Hicks: former NFL running back.

Janice B. Howroyd: founder and CEO of ACT-1 Group.

Jesse Jackson Sr.: civil rights activist and founder and CEO of Rainbow Push Coalition.

Jesse Jackson Jr.: congressman, Illinois.

Jonathan Jackson: civil rights activist, businessman, and professor.

Robert Jackson: former NFL player and first player from an HBCU to be drafted in the NFL.

Jamal Jones: former NFL wide receiver.

Henrv Frye: first black justice and chief justice of North Carolina Supreme Court.

Ronald McNair: NASA astronaut, died in the Space Shuttle Challenger explosion in 1986.

Mel Phillips: former NFL player and currently Miami Dolphins's coach.

J. D. Smith: former NFL running back.

Edolphus Towns: Congressman from New York.

Jake Wheatley: member of the Pennsylvania House of Representatives.

Terrence J.: radio and TV personality.

North Carolina Central University

History

NCCU is a public, historically black university in the University of North Carolina System. Located in Durham, NC, it offers programs at the baccalaureate, master's, professional, and doctoral levels. The university is a member-school of the Thurgood Marshall College Fund. NCCU was founded by James E. Shepard as the National Religious Training School and Chautauqua in the Haiti District. It was chartered in 1909 as a private institution and opened in 1910 as a private institution. The school was sold and reorganized in 1915, becoming the National Training School. Becoming a state-funded institution in 1923, it was renamed the North Carolina College for Negroes. It was the nation's first state-supported, liberal arts college for black students. The college was accredited by the Southern Association of Colleges and Secondary Schools as an "A" class institution in 1937, but it was not admitted to membership until 1957. In 1947, the General Assembly changed the name of the institution to North Carolina College at Durham. In 1969, the General Assembly designated the institution as one of the state's regional universities, and the name was changed to NCCU.

Relevant Information

Established: 1910

Type: Public, HBUC

Location: 1801 Fayetteville St., Durham, NC 27707

Phone: 919-530-6100

Religious Affiliation: NA

Student Enrollment: 8,612

Tuition Fees: In-state $5,478; out-of-state $15,088

Academic Staff: 390

Campus: Urban, 135 acres

School Colors: Maroon and gray

Mascot/Nickname: Eagles

Athletics/Sports Affiliation: NCAA Div. I, MEAC

Endowment: $19,282,264

Notable Alumni

Evelyn Smalls: president and CEO of United Bank of Philadelphia.

Jason Smoots: professional track athlete.

James Speed: president and CEO of North Carolina Mutual Life Insurance Company.

André L. Talley: editor-at-large, *Vogue* magazine.

Cressie Thigpen: North Carolina Court of Appeals.

Earlie Thorpe: prominent historian and educator.

Doug Wilkerson: former professional football player.

Paul Winslow: former professional football player.

Arenda L. W. Allen: judge of US District Court of Virginia.

Yahzarah: singer.

David Young: former professional basketball player.

Ernie Warlick: former AFL and CFL professional football player.

Sunshine Anderson: singer.

Herman Boone: former high school football coach, profiled in the motion picture *Remember the Times*.

Frank Ballance: former member of US North Carolina House of Representatives.

Ernie Barnes: artist and former professional football player.

Larry Black: Olympic track and field gold and silver medalist.

Dan Blue: North Carolina Speaker of the House and president of National Conference of State Legislatures.

Julia Boseman: North Carolina senator.

Jim Brewington: former professional football player.

Wanda G. Bryant: North Carolina Court of Appeals jurist.

G. K. Butterfield: congressman and former associated justice, North Carolina Supreme Court.

Phonte Coleman: rapper.

Kim Coles: comedian and actress.

Julius L. Chambers: lawyer, civil rights leader, educator, and past president of NCCU.

Eva M. Clayton: former member of US House of Representatives, North Carolina.

Lee Davis: former professional ABA all-star player.

Ivan Dixon: actor.

Walter Douglas: CEO of Avis Ford.

Mike Easley: former governor of North Carolina.

Rick Elmore: North Carolina Court of Appeals jurist.

Kevin Foy: mayor of Chapel Hill, NC.

Willie E. Gary: attorney, motivational speaker, and cable TV executive.

George Hamilton: president of Dow Automotive.

Charles "Tex" Harrison: former Harlem Globetrotters' coach and player.

Bill Hayes: former head football coach at Winston-Salem State and A&T State Universities.

Audwin Helton: president and CEO of Spatial Data Integrations, Inc.

Maynard Jackson: first black mayor of Atlanta, GA.

Gene C. Jarmon: General Counsel of Texas Department of Insurance.

Sam Jones: NBA Hall of Fame.

Vernon Jones: politician and former CEO of DeKalb County, GA.

Eleanor Kinnaird: member of North Carolina Senate.

Clarence Lightner: first black mayor of Raleigh, NC.

Bishop Eddie Long: senior pastor of New Birth Missionary Baptist Church, Lithonia, GA.

Jeanne Lucas: first black elected to the North Carolina Senate.

Crystal G. Mangum: dancer.

Robert Massey: former NFL defensive back and current head football coach at Shaw University.

Henry "Mickey" Michaux: member of North Carolina House of Representatives.

Levelle Moton: former professional basketball player.

Greg Peterson: former professional football player.

Charles Romes: former professional football player.

Leon Rouson: former National Black Teacher of the Year.

Rashaun D. Rucker: national Emmy-winning photojournalist and first black to be named Michigan Press Photographer of the Year.

Julius Sang: former Summer Olympics track athlete.

OAKWOOD UNIVERSITY

History

Oakwood University is a private university located in Huntsville, AL. It is owned and operated by the Seventh-day Adventist Church. A group of college constituents made the decision in 2007 to change the school's name from Oakwood College to Oakwood University. It is a member of the UNCF. Oakwood University is accredited by the SACS and the Department of Education of the General Conference of Seventh-day Adventists to award the associate, baccalaureate, and master's degrees. The university has performed well in external rankings, having listed among the Best Baccalaureate Colleges in the Southern Regions numbering 31 and 28 on the list of Best Historically Black Colleges and Universities, tied with Alabama A&M University and the University of Maryland Eastern Shore (UMES). The university is also listed on a regular basis among the top twenty institutions of higher learning that provide African Americans to medical schools.

Relevant Information

Established: 1896

Type: Private, HBCU

Location: 7000 Adventist Blvd., NW, Huntsville, AL 35896

Phone: 256-726-7000

Religious Affiliation: Seventh-day Adventist

Student Enrollment: 1,810

Tuition Fees: In-state and out-of-state $15,412

Academic Staff: NA

Campus: Suburban, 1,185 acres

School Colors: Blue and gold

Mascot/Nickname: Ambassadors

Athletics/Sports Affiliations: USCAA

Endowment: $8,514,297

Notable Alumni

Delbert Baker: administrator, educator, author, and president of Oakwood University.

Ishakamusa Barashango: college professor and lecturer in Afrocentrism and founder of Temple of the Black Messiah.

Barry Black: former US Navy chief of chaplains and chaplain of the US Senate.

Ronald Brise: Florida State Representative.

Angela Brown: soprano opera singer.

Alvin Chea: member of the gospel group "Take 6."

Clifton Davis: actor, pastor, and songwriter.

Hallerin H. Hill: radio talk show host, WNOX, Knoxville, TN.

T. R. M. Howard: civil rights leader, surgeon, entrepreneur, mentor to Medgar Evers and Fannie Lou Hamer.

Heather Knight: president of Pacific Union College.

Brian McKnight: R&B singer/musician and brother of alumnus Claude McKnight.

Claude McKnight: member of the gospel group "Take 6."

Toni Neal: traffic anchor, WSB-TV, Atlanta, GA.

Wintley Phipps: pastor, singer, founder, and president of US Dream Academy.

John F. Street: mayor of Philadelphia.

Mervyn Warren: member of the gospel group "Take 6."

Amber Bullock: winner of Season 4 BET's *Sunday Best*.

PAINE COLLEGE

History

Paine College, formally Paine Institute, is a private, historically black college located in Augusta, GA. It was founded by the leadership of the Methodist Episcopal Church South—now United Methodist Church—and the Colored Methodist Episcopal Church—now CME Church. In 1882, the Paine College board of trustees met for the first time to name the school in honor of Bishop Robert Paine of the MECS, who organized the CME Church. The Paine Institute began with a high school component and gradually developed a college department. In 1901, the first four-year degrees were granted, and in 1903, the school's name was changed to Paine College. Paine was accredited by the SACS in 1961. Paine is a full-fledged liberal arts institution offering courses and major programs in five divisions: business administration, education, humanities, natural sciences, and mathematics and social sciences. The college remains a small predominantly black, coeducational, church-related school and opens to all.

Relevant Information

Established: 1882

Type: Private, HBCU

Location: 1235 15th St., Augusta, GA 30901

Phone: 706-821-8200

Religious Affiliation: United Methodist Church

Student Enrollment: 900

Tuition Fees: $11,550

Academic Staff: NA

Campus: Urban, 57 acres

School Colors: White and blue

Mascot/Nickname: Urban

Athletics/Sports Affiliation: NCAA Div. II and SIAC

Endowment: $12 million

Notable Alumni

Channing Tobias: civil rights activist and appointee on President's Committee on Civil Rights.

William H. Harris: past president of Paine College, TSU, and Alabama State University.

Mack Gipson Jr.: NASA consultant and second African American to obtain a PhD in geology.

Emma A. Gresham: mayor of Keysville, GA.

Shirley McBay: first African American dean at Massachusetts Institute of Technology.

Nathaniel Linsey: senior bishop of CME Church.

Ruth B. Crawford: director of Shiloh Community Center and designer of the Paine College flag.

Mike Thurmond: attorney and first African American elected as Georgia Labor Commissioner.

John W. Gilbert: first African American archaeologist.

Lucius Pitts: first African American president of Paine College.

Elias Blake: HBCU advocate who helped to develop the Upward Bound Program and past president of Clark College.

Micah Troy: hip-hop musician known as "Pastor Troy."

Joseph Lowery: president of Southern Christian Leadership Conference.

Woodie W. White: bishop of the United Methodist Church.

Frank Yerby: internationally acclaimed author and film writer.

PAUL QUINN COLLEGE

History

Paul Quinn College is a private, historically black college (HBCU) located on 144 acres just south of downtown Dallas, TX. The college is affiliated with the AME Church. Paul Quinn College holds the distinction of being the oldest historically black college west of the Mississippi River. The college was founded in 1872 in Austin, TX, by a small group of AME preachers at Metropolitan AME Church. Originally, the college was the Connectional High School and Institute. In 1877, the college moved from Austin to Waco, TX, and was renamed Waco College. The college relocated to Dallas, TX. It acquired the former campus of Bishop College. In May 1881, the college was chartered by the State of Texas and changed its name to Paul Quinn College to commemorate the contributions of Bishop William Paul Quinn.

Relevant Information

Established: 1872

Type: Private, HBCU

Location: 3837 Simpson Stuart Rd., Dallas, TX 75241

Phone: 214-376-1000

Religious Affiliation: AME Church

Student Enrollment: 198

Tuition Fees: $12,350

Academic Staff: NA

Campus: Urban, 142 acres

School Colors: Purple and gold

Mascot/Nickname: Tigers and Quinnites

Athletics/Sports Affiliations: NAIA, RRAC

Endowment: NA

Notable Alumni

Dick Campbell: theater producer and director in New York, who helped to launch the career of Ossie Davis.

Christopher Saunders: sports broadcaster for ZNS-TV-13 in the Bahamas.

Mims Hackett: former politician who served in the New Jersey General Assembly.

Frank Sims: retired corporate vice president of Transportation & Supply Chain Solution, Cargill Incorporated.

Nuru Witherspoon: partner at Kelley Witherspoon, LLP.

Hiawatha Williams: entrepreneur and founder of Williams Chicken.

PHILANDER SMITH COLLEGE

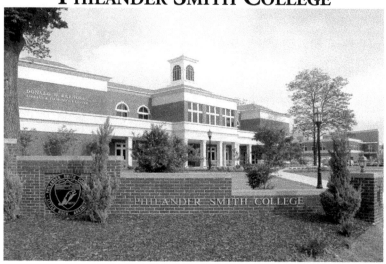

History

Philander Smith College is a historically black college and four-year undergraduate liberal arts institution located in Little Rock, AR. Philander Smith is affiliated with the United Methodist Church and a founding member of the UNCF.

The mission of Philander Smith College is to graduate academically accomplished students who are grounded for social justice. The college was officially founded in 1877 under the name of Walden Seminary as a means of providing educational opportunities for freed slaves west of the Mississippi River. The school was renamed Philander Smith in recognition of the financial contributions of Adeline Smith, the widow of Philander Smith. The college was chartered as a four-year college in 1983 and conferred its first bachelor's degree in 1888. The college was a pioneer during the civil rights movement as many of its students engaged in nonviolent resistance against segregation laws.

Relevant Information

Established: 1877

Type: Private, HBCU

Location: 900 W. Daisy L Gatson Bates Dr., Little Rock, AR 72202

Phone: 501-137-5987

Religious Affiliation: United Methodist Church

Student Enrollment: 600

Tuition Fees: $11,804

Academic Staff: NA

Campus: Urban, 25 acres

School Colors: Green and gold

Mascot/Nickname: Panthers

Athletics/Sports Affiliation: NAIA and GCAC

Endowment: $3 million

Notable Alumni

"Geese" Ausbie: former Harlem Globetrotters player and coach.

James H. Cone: major figure in systematic theology and liberation theology.

Joycelyn Elders: former surgeon general of United States.

Calvin King: farm developer and president of the Arkansas Land and Farm Development Corporation.

Lottie Shackelford: former mayor of Little Rock, AR.

Elijah Pitts: former Green Bay Packers player.

AI Bell: founder of Stax Records and former president of Motown Records.

Robert L. Williams: prominent figure in the history of African American psychology.

PRAIRIE VIEW A&M UNIVERSITY

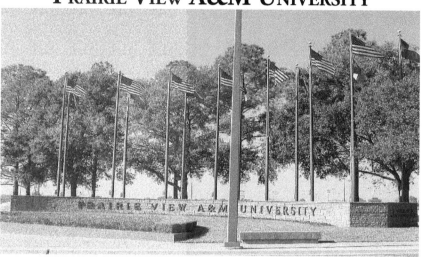

History

Prairie View A&M University (PVAMU) is a historically black university located in Prairie View, TX, USA, northwest of Houston, and is a member of the Texas A&M University System. PVAMU offers baccalaureate degrees in fifty academic majors, thirty-seven master's degrees, and four doctoral degree programs through nine colleges and schools. PVAMU is one of the Texas's land-grant universities. The university is a member-school of the Thurgood Marshall College Fund. Founded in 1876, PVAMU is the second oldest state-sponsored institution of higher education in Texas. The state legislature, consistent with the terms of the federal Morrill Land-Grant Colleges Act, authorized an "Agricultural and Mechanical College for the benefit of Colored Youth." In 1945, the name of the institution was changed from Prairie View Normal and Industrial College to Prairie View A&M College of Texas, followed by the name of PVAMU in 1973.

Relevant Information

Established: 1876

Type: Public, HBCU

Location: 5th St. Ave. AL W. Minor St., Prairie View, Tx. 77446

Phone: 936-261-3311

Religious Affiliation: NA

Student Enrollment: 8,608

Tuition Fees: In-state $18,726; out-of-state $29,116

Academic Staff: 422

Campus: Rural, 1,502 acres

School Colors: Purple and gold

Mascot/Nickname: Panthers

Athletics/Sports Affiliation: NCAA Div. I, SWAC

Endowment: $54,144,181

Notable Alumni

Julius W. Becton Jr.: lieutenant general of the US Army, educator, past president of PVAMU.

J. Don Boney: first president of the University of Houston-Downtown.

Charlie Brackins: former NFL quarterback.

David L. Brewer: retired vice admiral of the US Navy.

Charles Brown: legendary blues recording artist.

Emanuel Cleaver: US Representative of Missouri.

Cecil Cooper: five-time Major League All-Star with Boston Red Sox and Milwaukee Brewers.

D. J. Premier: member of Gang Starr.

Dorrough: rapper.

Wendel Eckford: first African American to earn PhD in history at Claremont Graduate University, CA.

Terry Ellis: vocalist and member of female R&B group En Vogue.

Clement E. Glenn: Democratic candidate for Texas Governor.

Adrian Hamilton: current NFL linebacker.

Ken Houston: member of Pro Football Hall of Fame.

Louise D. Hutchinson: historian.

Jim Kearney: former NFL defensive back.

Jermaine McGhee: former NFL defensive lineman.

Sidney A. McPhee: president of Middle TSU.

Dellenor Miles: vocalist/actress.

OG Ron C: DJ record executor.

Frederick D. Patterson: founder of UNCF.

Inez B. Prosser: first African American woman to receive a doctoral degree in psychology.

Bmer Aedd: head coach, Lufkin Dunbar High, PVIL Division 3A State Football Championships.

Dewey Redman: jazz saxophonist.

Mr. T: actor.

Otis Taylor: member of 1969 World Champion Kansas City Chiefs Hall of Fame.

Calvin Walker: US Army General.

Craig Washington: former US House of Representative from Texas.

Dave Webster: former AFL all-pro football player.

Hise Austin: former NFL wide receiver.

Kirko Bangz: rapper.

Sebastian Barrie: former NFL defensive lineman.

Zelmo Beaty: former NBA basketball player for St. Louis Hawks, Atlanta Hawks, and Utah Stars.

RUST COLLEGE

History

Rust College is a historically black, liberal arts college located in Holly Springs, MS. Located approximately 35 miles southeast of Memphis, TN, it is the second oldest private college in the state. Affiliated with the United Methodist Church, it is one of the historically black colleges and universities founded before 1868 that is still operating. Rust was founded in 1866 by Northern missionaries with a group called the Freedmen's Aid Society of the Methodist Episcopal Church. In 1870, the college was chartered as Shaw University, honoring Rev. S. 0. Shaw, who made a gift of $10,000 to the institution. In 1882 the institution changed its name to Rust University, a tribute to Richard S. Rust, the secretary of the Freedmen's Aid Society.

Rust College is the oldest of the eleven historically black colleges and universities related to the United Methodist Church, the second oldest private college in Mississippi, and one of the five historically black colleges that was founded before 1867.

Relevant Information

Established: 1866

Type: Private, HBCU

Location: 150 Rust Ave., Holly Springs, MS 38635

Phone: 662-252-8000

Religious Affiliation: United Methodist Church

Student Enrollment: 1,200-

Tuition Fees: In-state and out-of-state approx. $14,000

Academic Staff: NA

Campus: Rural, 126 acres

School Colors: Royal blue and white

Mascot/Nickname: Bearcats

Athletics/Sports Affiliation: NCAA Div. Ill

Endowment: NA

Notable Alumni

Alexander P. Shaw: Methodist and notable preacher.

Ruby Elzy: pioneer opera singer who created the role Serena in *Porgy and Bess.*

Perry W. Howard: African American politician and member of Republican National Committee.

Clinton LeSueur: journalist.

Ida B. Wells: newspaper editor, feminist, and anti-lynching crusader.

Anita Ward: African American singer of disco hit "Ring My Bell."

SAVANNAH STATE UNIVERSITY

History

Savannah State University is a four-year, state-supported, historically black university (HBCU) located in Savannah, GA. Savannah State University is the oldest public historically black university in Georgia. Savannah University's mission statement is to graduate students who are prepared to perform at higher levels of economic productivity, social responsibility, and excellence in their chosen career fields of endeavor in changing a global community. The university is a member-school of the Thurgood Marshall College Fund. Savannah State University was originally founded as a result of the Second Morrill Land-Grant Act of August 1890. The Georgia General Assembly passed legislature creating the Georgia Industrial College for Colored Youth. The school operated in Atlanta, GA, in 1891 before moving to its permanent location in Athens. From a normal school, it was converted to a full college with a four-year curriculum. With the growth in its graduate and research programs, the college became a full-member institution of the University System of Georgia, and its name was changed to Savannah State College, and in 1950, the college changed its name to Savannah State University.

Relevant Information

Established: 1890

Type: Public, HBCU

Location: 3219 College St., Savannah, GA 31404

Phone: 912-358-4778

Religious Affiliation: NA

Student Enrollment: 4,552

Tuition Fees: Not Available

Academic Staff: 385

Campus: Coastal setting, 175 acres

School Colors: Burnt orange and reflex blue

Mascot/Nickname: Tigers

Athletics/Sports Affiliation: MEAC, NCAA Div. I

Endowment: $2,433,508

Notable Alumni

George E. Kent: professor of Afro-American literature.

Charles Elmore: African American scholar and jazz historian.

Jerome Miller: vice president of Toyota Motor Sales.

Curtis Cooper: Savannah-area civil rights leader.

W. W. Law: nationally known civil rights leader.

Edna P. Jackson: member of National League of Cities.

Barbara J. Mobley: former member of the DeKalb County Georgia State Court bench and former member of Georgia House of Representatives.

Alissa J. Johnson: deputy chief information officer of Executive Office of President Obama's office.

Donnie Cochran: retired US Navy captain with the Blue Angels.

Walter E. Gaskin: major general, US Marine Corps.

James E. Wright: former flight instructor for World War II Tuskegee Airmen.

JaQuitta Williams: former anchor/reporter for WSEHV, ABC affiliate, Atlanta, GA.

Steven Aycock: head football coach at Johnson C. Smith.

Bobby Curtis: former NFL player for Washington Redskins and New York Jets.

Roy Ellison: NFL official and umpire.

Troy Hambrick: former NFL running back.

Matt Jackson: former member of Harlem Globetrotters.

Jessie Kenlaw: interim head coach of WNBA's Washington Mystics and assistant coach with WNBA Seattle Storm.

John Mathis: former ABA forward for New Jersey Americans.

Wesley McGriff: defensive coach for Vanderbilt Commodores and Miami Hurricanes.

Ernest Miller: former professional wrestler.

Shannon Sharpe: former NFL player and three-time Super Bowl Champion.

SELMA UNIVERSITY

History

Selma University is a private, historically black, Bible college located in Selma, AL. It is affiliated with the Alabama State Missionary Baptist Convention. The institution was founded in 1873 as the Alabama Baptist Normal and Theological School to train African Americans as ministers and teachers. In 1881, the school was incorporated by an act of the legislature under the name of Alabama Baptist Normal and Theological School of Selma. The name was officially changed to Selma University. In the 1980s, Selma developed from a four-year bachelor's program in religion and two-year program in liberal arts to a four-year institution. In the autumn of 2000, Selma began its transformation from a Christian liberal arts college to a Bible college. In February 2009, Selma received initial accreditation from the Commission on Accreditation of the Association for Biblical Higher Education in Canada and the United States.

Relevant Information

Established: 1878

Type: Private, HBCU

Location: 1501 Lapsley St., Selma, AL 36701

Phone: 334-872-2533

Religious Affiliation: Alabama State Missionary Baptist Convention

Student Enrollment: 600

Tuition Fees: In-state $4,600, out-of-state $5,250

Academic Staff: NA

Campus: Remote setting, 36 acres

School Colors: Blue and white

Mascot/Nickname: NA

Athletics/Sports Affiliations: NA

Endowment: NA

Notable Alumni

Rickdrieka Sanders: NA.

Tara Neely: NA.

SHAW UNIVERSITY

History

Shaw University, founded as Raleigh institute, is a private, liberal arts institution, and historically black university in Raleigh, NC. Founded in 1885, it is the oldest HBCU in the Southern United States. Shaw is affiliated with the General Baptist State Convention of North Carolina and a member of the National Baptist Convention, USA, Inc., which supports the Shaw University Divinity School. It was renamed Shaw Collegiate Institute after Elijah Shaw, benefactor of Shaw Hall, the first building. In 1875, it became Shaw University. Leonard Medical School was established in 1881 as a part of the university, becoming the first four-year medical school in the South to train black doctors and pharmacists. By 1900, more than 30,000 black teachers had been trained. Shaw University has been called the mother of African American colleges in North Carolina. By the mid-1980s enrollment declined, and the university was deeply in debt. In the 1990s, Shaw ran a successful capital campaign to renovate historical buildings and to construct new campus facilities.

Relevant Information

Established: 1865

Type: Private, HBCU

Location: 118 East South St., Raleigh, NC 27601

Phone: 919-154-8569

Religious Affiliation: National Baptist Convention, USA

Student Enrollment: 2,800

Tuition Fees: $13,226

Academic Staff: 200

Campus: Urban, 30 acres

School Colors: Garnet and white

Mascot/Nickname: Bears

Athletics/Sports Affiliation: NCAA Div. II, CIAA

Endowment: $23 million

Notable Alumni

Ida V. Smith: one of the first African American female pilots and flight instructors in the United States.

William G. Pearson: educator and businessman, cofounder of Mechanics & Farmers Bank in Raleigh, NC.

James Smith: first heavyweight boxing champion with a college.

Rita Walters: currently on the Board of Library Commissioners for Los Angeles Public Library.

Lucius Walker: Baptist minister best known for his opposition to US embargo against Cuba.

Col. James H. Young: first African American to hold the rank of colonel in the US Army during the Spanish-American War.

Richard G. Arno: founder of the National Christian Counselors Association.

Ella Baker: leader of SNCC and civil rights activist.

Charlie Brandon: Grey Cup champion and all-star CFL football player.

Angie Brooks: former president of the United Nations General Assembly.

Shirley Caesar: pastor and gospel music artist.

Henry P. Cheatham: Republican member of the US House of Representatives.

James E. Cheek: former president of Shaw and Howard Universities.

Willie E. Gary: multimillionaire attorney and cofounder of the Black Family Channel.

Edward A. Johnson: first African American member of the New York State Legislature.

Lee Johnson: president and CEO of Mechanics & Farmers Bank.

Luther Jordan: former member of the North Carolina Senate.

Vernon Malone: member of North Carolina General Assembly.

Lee Monroe: president of Voorhees College.

Peter W. Moore: first president of Elizabeth City Normal College (now Elizabeth City State University (ECSU)).

Shelia P. Moses: author.

Ronald Murray: professional basketball player.

Eleanor Nunn: civil rights activist and one of the founders of SNCC.

William L. Pollard: president of Medgar Evers College.

M. T. Pope: prominent physician in Raleigh, NC.

Benjamin A. Quarles: historian, administrator, scholar, educator, and writer.

James E. Shepard: founder and president of North Carolina Central University (NCCU).

SHORTER UNIVERSITY

History

Shorter College was founded in 1873 as a women's college known as the Cherokee Baptist Female College. The college was renamed in 1877 to Shorter Female College because of financial contributions by Alfred and Martha Shorter. In the 1950s, the college became coeducational. The late 1950s saw the first African American student graduates. The political and social climate of the 1960s had a great effect on the college throughout the decade. International programs began in the 1950s, and the school expanded MBA programs. In 2005, the college attempted to break away from the Georgia Baptist Convention citing among other complaints fear of losing accreditation. The Georgia Supreme Court ruled that Shorter's board didn't have the authority to sever ties with the convention. In June 2010, Shorter College changed its name to reflect the institution's growth and expansion.

Relevant Information

Established: 1873

Type: Private, HBCU

Location: 315 Shorter Ave. SW, Rome, GA 30165

Phone: 706-129-2121

Religious Affiliation: Georgia Baptist Convention

Student Enrollment: 3,702

Tuition: $19,300 per year

Academic Staff: 388

Campus: Suburban, 150 acres

School Colors: White, Columbia blue and gold

Mascot/Nickname: Hawks

Athletics/Sports Affiliation: NCAA Div. II, GSC

Endowment: $27 million

Notable Alumni

J. Buxte Max: concert organist.

Vivian L. Aunspaugh: Texas painter and art teacher.

Marilyn Lloyd: Tennessee business woman and politician.

Nathan Dean: politician.

Jamie Barton: opera singer.

Bill Foster: head basketball coach in the NCAA.

Phil Jones: football coach of the year 2008 FCA Grant Teaff and AFCA regional.

Anthony O'Garro: professional soccer player.

SHELTON STATE COMMUNITY COLLEGE

History

Shelton State Community College is a two-year community college located in Tuscaloosa, AL. The Tuscaloosa Trade School was created in 1950. The school was renamed J. P. Shelton Trade School, which was renamed Shelton State Technical College.

In 1975, Brewer State Junior College (now Bevill State Community College) opened a branch campus in Tuscaloosa. Shelton State Community College was established in 1979 by the State Board of Education. In 1976, the merging of the schools created the Shelton State Community College consisting of two campuses: the Martin and Fredd campuses. Shelton is considered a historically black college.

Relevant Information

Established: 1952

Type: Community, HBCU

Location: 9500 Old Greensboro Rd., Tuscaloosa, AL 35405

Phone: 205-391-2211

Religious Affiliation: NA

Student Enrollment: 7,000

Tuition Fees: Annual cost $21,880

Academic Staff: 78

Campus Type and size: Suburban/Urban, 177 acres

School Colors: Gold and emerald

Mascot/Nickname: Buccaneers

Athletics/Sports Affiliation: NJCAA and ACCC

Endowment: NA

Notable Alumni

Fitzgerald Washington: general sales manager of Buffalo Rock Co., Tuscaloosa Distribution Center.

Others: NA

SOUTH CAROLINA STATE UNIVERSITY

History

South Carolina State University is a historically black university located in Orangeburg, SC. It is the only state-funded, historically black, land-grant institution in South Carolina and is a member of the Thurgood Marshall College Fund. Founded in 1896 as the state's only public college for blacks, the university has played a key role in the education of African Americans in the state and nation. The university has educated scores of teachers for the public. The support of the Rosenwald Fund and the General Education Board helped the institution to survive the Depression. After World War II, the state legislature created a graduate and a law school at the university to prevent black students from enrolling in the University of South Carolina's graduate and legal education programs. Since 1966, South Carolina State University has been opened to white students and faculty, but it has largely maintained its mission and character as a historically black institution. Today, there are nearly 5,000 students majoring in a wide range of programs.

Relevant Information

Established: 1896

Type: Public, HBCU

Location: 300 College Ave., Orangeburg, SC 29115

Phone: 803-260-5956

Religious Affiliation: NA

Student Enrollment: 5,000

Tuition Fees: NA

Academic Staff: 550

Campus: Urban, 447 acres

School Colors: Garnet and blue

Mascot/Nickname: Bulldogs

Athletics/Sports Affiliation: NCAA Div. I, MEAC

Endowment: $5 million

Notable Alumni

Richard G. Shaw: first African American who served as insurance commissioner in West Virginia.

Nefertari I. Baraka: award-winning educator, author, and Internet radio host.

Essie M. Washington Williams: educator and African American daughter of former US Senator Strom Thurmond.

Leroy Davis: former South Carolina state president.

Benjamin E. Mays: minister, educator, scholar, social activist, former president of Morehouse College.

M. Maceo Nance: former South Carolina state president.

Benjamin F. Payton: retired president of Tuskegee.

Andrew Hugine Jr.: former South Carolina state president and current president of Alabama A&M University.

M. C. Brown II: current president of Alcorn State University.

George c. Bradley: current president of Paine College.

Ron Westray: jazz trombonist, composer, and educator.

Shombay Kimoni: author, entrepreneur, and artist.

Doug Stewart: co-host of sports talk radio show of the *2 Live Stews*.

Armstrong Williams: conservative talk show host and commentator.

Juanita Goggins: first African American woman elected to the South Carolina Legislature.

James E. Clyburn: US Representative from South Carolina and majority whip in US Congress.

Ernest A. Finney Jr.: first African American Supreme Court judge appointed to South Carolina Supreme Court since Reconstruction Era.

Matthew J. Perry: US Federal judge.

Clifford L. Stanley: US Undersecretary of Defense for Personnel and Readiness.

Amos M. Gailllard Jr.: retired brigadier general in the New York Guard.

George B. Price: retired brigadier general in the US Army.

Abraham J. Turner: retired major general in the US Army.

Stephen Twitty: brigadier general in the US Army.

Henry Doctor Jr.: retired lieutenant general in the US Army.

Willie Jeffries: legendary college football coach at South Carolina State and. Howard Universities.

Deacon Jones: former professional football player; inducted into Pro Football Hall of Fame.

Phillip Adams: current NFL defensive back.

Willie Aikens: former Major League baseball player.

Rickey Anderson: former National Football League running back.

Orlando Brawn: former professional football player for Cleveland Browns and Baltimore Ravens.

Rafael Bush: current NFL defensive back.

Barney Bussey: former National Football League running back.

Harry Carson: former professional football player for New York Giants and Pro Football Hall of Fame.

Barney Chavous: former NFL defensive end.

Chartric Dalby: professional football player for Tampa Bay Buccaneers and Seattle Seahawks.

James Lee: professional football player for Tampa Bay Buccaneers.

Arthur Love: former NFL tight end for the New England Patriots.

Philip J. Murphy: former professional football player for Los Angeles Rams and principal for P. J. Murphy Co. Investment Banking Services.

Robert Porcher: former NFL defensive end Detroit Lions.

Raleigh Roundtree: former NFL player.

Donnie Shell: former professional football player for Pittsburgh Steelers.

Mickey Sims: former professional football player for Cleveland Browns.

SOUTHERN UNIVERSITY SYSTEM

History

Southern University is a historically black college located in Baton Rouge, LA. The Baton Rouge campus is located on Scott's Bluff overlooking the Mississippi River in the northern section of the city of Baton Rouge. Thecity parish has a population of more than 500,000 and serves as a cultural, political, educational, and industrial center for South Louisiana. The campus includes an agricultural experimental station on an additional 372-acre site, located 5 miles north of the main campus. The university is a member of the Thurgood Marshall College Fund. The institution continued to grow, and in 1974, a special session of the Louisiana Legislature established the Southern University System. The system consisted of Southern University and A&M College in Baton Rouge (main campus), Southern University at New Orleans, Southern University at Shreveport, Southern University Law Center in Baton in Baton Rouge, and Southern University Agricultural Research and Extension Center in Baton Rouge. The university was one of the first historically black colleges to receive a visit from first Lady, Eleanor Roosevelt, in 1943.

Relevant Information

Established: 1880

Type: land-grant, HBCU

Location: 801 Harding Blvd., Baton Rouge, LA 70807

Phone: 225-771-4500

Religious Affiliation: NA

Student Enrollment: 7,313

Tuition Fees: In-state, $5,074; out-of-state $11,612

Academic Staff: 1,465

Campus: Urban, 964 acres

School Colors: Columbia Blue and gold

Mascot/Nickname: Jaguars

Athletics/Sports Affiliation: NCAA Div. l, SWAG

Endowment: $9.6 million

Notable Alumni

Rich Jackson: member of American Football League Hall of Fame.

Mel Blount: member of American Pro Football League Hall of Fame.

Lou Brock: record-setting base-stealing Major League baseball player.

Harold Carmichael: four-time NFL Pro Bowler.

Willie Davenort: two-time gold medalist of US Olympic Track Team.

Trenidad Hubbard: former Major League baseball player.

Marvin Davis: former NFL and CFL player and Grey Cup champion.

Kip Holden: mayor-president of Baton Rouge since 2005.

Avery Johnson: 2006 NBA Coach of the Year.

Ralph W. Jones: president and baseball coach at Grambling State University (GSU).

Tyron Jones: former Canadian Football League all-star and MVP.

Fred Lewis: current Major League baseball player.

Bob Love: former NBA all-star.

Rod Milburn: track and field gold medalist at 1972 Munich Olympic Games.

Jordan Miller: current NFL defensive tackle.

Bobby Phills: NBA basketball player.

lsiah Robertson: six-time NFL Pro Bowler.

Bernie Smith: former Major League baseball player.

Donnell Smith: NFL player.

Godwin Turk: former NFL player.

Rickie Weeks: current Major League baseball player.

Aeneas Williams: former NFL Pro Bowler.

Jerry Wilson: former NFL player.

Alvin Batiste: jazz artist and educator

lsiah Cary: television news reporter

Maurice Brown: jazz artist

Lavell Crump: music recording artist

Thaddeus Ford: jazz musician

Randy Jackson: musician, record producer and American IDOL judge

Branford Marsalis: jazz Saxophonist

Terysa Singleton: Miss Black Louisiana USA- 2006-2007

Brittany Brown: Miss Black Louisiana USA - 2009-2011

Nesby Phips: record producer and hip hop artist

Kirt Bennett: African-American Republican candidate for lieutenant governor in 2003

Jay Blossman: former member of the Louisiana Public Service Commission

lrma M. Dixon: first African American elected to the Louisiana Public Service Commission

Cleo Fields: representative, U.S. Congress

Hunter Greene: Republican member of the Louisiana House of Representatives

Melvin Holden: first African-American mayor of Baton Rouge, La.

William J. Jefferson: former Representative, U.S. Congress

Okla Jones: Federal judge on U.S. District Court

lsiah Leggett: county Executive of Montgomery County, Maryland

Robert M. Marionneaux: Louisiana State senator from Baton Rouge area

Abe E. Pierce: first African American mayor of mayor of Monroe. La.

Chris Roy, Jr. Attorney: state legislator from Rapides and Vernon parishes

Jessie N. Stone: attorney; educator and Dean of Southern University Law Center and as president of Southern University

Thomas T. Townsend: member of Louisiana House of Representatives, 2Q00-2008

-Pinkie C. Wilkerson: member of Louisiana House of Representatives, 1992-2000

Tom Willmott: member of Louisiana House of Representatives, since 2008

Sherian G. Cadoria: brigadier General (retired), First female African American to reach in U.S. Army

Russel L. Honore: lieutenant General who commanded U.S. military recovery support after Katrina and Rita

Joe N. Ballard: lieutenant General (retired) First African-American Chief of Engineers of U.S Corps of Engineers

Jody Amedee: (1995) Louisiana state senator from District 18

Sherman Q. Mack: (1999) Louisiana District 95 state representative

Louis Moore: federal Magistrate Judge on U.S. District Court of Louisiana

Willie Hunter, Jr.: former Louisiana State Representative

Annette M. Eddie-Callagain: first African American to have a private law practice in Japan.

John M. Guidry: judge of First Circuit of the Louisiana Courts of Appeal and former Louisiana State Senator

Claire Babineaux-Fontenot: senior vice president and chief tax officer for Walmart Stores, Inc.

Hillar C. Moore III: district attorney for the 19th Judicial District, Baton Rouge, La.

Marcus Hunter: member of the Louisiana House of Representatives

Rick Ward III: Louisiana state senator from District 17

Jonathan W. Perry: (1998) state representative from Vermilion and

Cameron parishes

Meshea Poore: member of the West Virginia House of Delegates Mike Foster: (2004) former Governor of Louisiana

Faith Jenkins: Miss Louisiana, Miss America 2001 first runner-up, attorney

and legal analyst.

SOUTHWESTERN CHRISTIAN COLLEGE

History

Southwestern Christian College (SwCC) was founded in 1948 under the name Southern Bible Institute in Fort Worth, TX, with an initial class of forty-five students. In 1949, the school purchased the property of the closed Texas Military College and relocated the campus, at that time it took its present name. The campus occupies two locally historical facilities. The first dwelling erected in Terrell, TX, an octagonal-shaped house; despite its shape, it is called the "Round House" to give better protection against Indians.

It is one of only twenty surviving Round Houses in the entire nation. SwCC became accredited by the SACS in 1973 and is currently accredited to award associate and bachelor-level degrees. Two years of study in most fields are offered outside of those involving preparation for full-time ministry.

Relevant Information

Established: 1948

Type: Private, HBCU

Location: 200 Bowser Cir. Terrell, TX 75160

Phone: 972-152-3341

Religious Affiliation: Churches of Christ

Student Enrollment: 224

Tuition Fees: $15,491 per year

Academic Staff: NA

Campus: NA

School Colors: White and blue

Mascot/Nickname: Rams

Athletics/Sports Affiliation: NJCAA Div. I

Endowment: NA

Notable Alumni

Rayshan Booke: recorded rendition of Sam Cooke's "A Change is Gonna Come."

Rodney Dulin: senior minister of Central Pointe Church, Dallas, TX.

Phillip Edwards: assistant director of "Summer Tour" and first all-male ensemble to record "Amen" at SwCC.

Jeannette G. Gibbs: award-winning teacher in the Terrell Independent School District.

Fate Hagood Ill: senior minister of Metropolitan Church of Christ in Los Angeles, CA.

Jacqueline W. Jernigan: senior budget analyst of Army Corps of Engineers.

Bennett Johnson Jr.: treasurer of Dallas Area Dinner Day Committee for SwCC.

Joie Rasberry: gifted public speaker and established Rasberry's House of Hope.

Stevie Roberts: superintendent and CEO of Miracle Education Systems in Houston, TX.

Sylvia Shanks: serves as general counsel for US Government

Accountability Office.

John Tillman Jr.: owner of several McDonalds in several Houston communities.

Gerald Turner: standout vocalist.

SPELMAN COLLEGE

History

Spelman College is a four-year, liberal arts women's college located in Atlanta, GA. The college is part of the Atlanta University Center academic consortium in Atlanta. Founded in 1881 as the Atlanta Baptist Female Seminary, Spelman was the first historically black female institution of higher education to receive its collegiate charter in 1924. It holds the distinction of being America's oldest historically black college for women. Spelman is ranked among the nation's top liberal arts colleges and universities for producing Fulbright Scholars, is the second largest producer of African American college graduates who attend medical school, is one of the nation's top ten women's colleges, and has been ranked among the best 373 colleges and universities in America.

Relevant Information

Established: 1881

Type: Private, HBCU

Location: 350 Spelman lane, SW, Atlanta, GA 30314

Phone: 404-168-3643

Religious Affiliation: Atlanta Baptist Female Seminary

223

Student Enrollment: 2500

Tuition Fees: In-state and out-of-state $23,794

Academic Staff: 174

Campus: Urban, 39 acres

School Colors: Blue and gold

Mascot/Nickname: Jaguars

Athletics/Sports Affiliation: NCAA Div. Ill

Endowment: $284.7 millions

Notable Alumni

Tina M. Ansa: author.

Blanche Armwood: educator and activist.

Angela M. Banks: professor of law at William & Mary Law School.

Mary Barksdale: past president of Jack and Jill.

J. Veronica Biggins: director of AirTran Airways and former director of Presidential Personnel in White House.

Traci L. Blackwell: vice president of Current Programming at the CW Television Network.

Janet Bragg: aviation pioneer.

Aurelia Brazeal: US Ambassador to Ethiopia and Kenya.

Rosalind G. Brewer: executive vice president of Walmart Stores, Inc.

Linda G. Bryant: documentary filmmaker (*Rag Wars*).

Selena S. Butler: founder of the first black Parent-Teacher Congress for Colored Parents and Teachers.

Pearl Cleage: novelist, playwright, poet, essayist, and journalist.

Betty Davis: meteorologist, formerly of The Weather Channel.

Cassi Davis: actress.

Renita B. Clark: notable physician in Detroit, MI.

Kimberly B. Davis: president of JP Morgan Chase Foundation.

Ruth A. Davis: twenty-fourth director general of US Foreign Service.

Phire Dawson: "Barker's Beauty" on The Price is Right.

Jerri DeVard: chief marketing officer at Nokia and former officer at Citigroup.

Dazon D. Diallo: founder/CEO of Sister Love, Inc.

Mattiwilda Dobbs: opera singer.

Marian W. Edelman: founder of Children's Defense Fund and won Presidential Medal of Freedom.

Mary M. Edmonds: vice provost and dean of Student Affairs Emeritus at Stanford University.

Christine King Farris: public speaker who teaches at Spelman College.

Virginia D. Royd: vice president of PROMETRA.

Mary A. Gordon: vice president of manufacturing at US Smokeless Tobacco Company.

Sheryl A. Gripper: four-time Emmy Award winner and founder of Black Women Rim Network.

Tia Fuller: saxophonist, composer, and educator.

Evelynn M. Hammonds: dean of Harvard College and professor of history of science at Harvard University.

Marcelite J. Harris: first African American female to obtain the rank of general in the US Air Force.

Celeste W. Hayes: professor of sociology and vice chair and director of Graduate Studies at Northwestern University.

Varnette Honeywood: creator of the Little Bill character. Clement Jackson: former national president of the YWCA.

Yvonne A. Jackson: former chief human resource official at three Fortune 500 companies.

Adrienne Joi Johnson: actress.

Clara S. Jones: first African American president of the American Library

Association.

Tayari Jones: author.

Alberta W. King: mother of Martin L. King, Jr.

Bernice King: president, SCLC and daughter of Martin L. King, Jr.

Audrey F. Manley: president emerita of Spelman College and former Acting Surgeon General of U. S.

Kathleen M. Anderson: television producer and playwright.

Tanya W. Pratt: judge, U.S. District Court.

Ruby Robinson: civil rights activist and executive secretary of SNCC.

Beverly G-Sheftall: author, feminist scholar and founder of Women's Research at Spelman College.

Deborah P – Stith: first female Commissioner of Public Health for Commonwealth of Massachusetts.

Keshia K. Pulliam: actress on The Cosby Show and House of Payne.

Tanika Ray: actress and TV personality.

Bernice J. Reagon, founder of Sweet Honey In the Rock; MacArthur Fellow; Professor Emeritus American Univ.

LaTanya Richardson: actress and wife of actor Samuel L. Jackson.

Esther Rolle: actress, Good Times.

Shaun Robinson: co-anchor, Access Hollywood; former host. TV One Access.

Nofiwe Rooks: Princeton University professor and author.

Dovey J. Roundtree: trail attorney, military veteran and civil rights pioneer.

Eva Rutland: author of more than 20 Romance novels.

Brenda V. Smith: law professor; appointed by Nancy Pelosi to the Nation Prison Rape Elimination Commission.

Sharmell Sullivan: Miss Black America, 1991, and wife of professional wrestler Booker T.

Sue B. Thurman: founder and first chairperson, National Council of

Negro Women's National Library.

Danica Tisdale: Miss Georgia, 2004, (first African American to hold the title).

Alice Walker: Pulitzer Prize winning novelist, The Color Purple

Rolonda Watts: journalist, actor, writer and former talk show host.

Elynor A. Williams: vice president of Public Responsibility at Sara Lee Corporation.

Ella G. Yate: first African American director of the Atlanta Fulton Public Library System.

Toni C. Bambara: author.

Pearl Cleage: author.

Jelani Cobb: author and Journalist.

Etta Z. Falconer: mathematician.

Gloria W. Gayles: author and founder of SIS Oral History Project.

Beverly G. Sheftall: author, feminist scholar, founder of Women's Research Center at Spelman College.

M. B. Kummba: author, feminist, activist.

Staughton Lynd: historian, activist, and attorney.

Ruby - Doris Smith Robinson: civil rights activist, SNCC executive and attorney

Howard Zinn: historian and civil rights activist

SAINT AUGUSTINE'S UNIVERSITY

History

Saint Augustine's University is a historically black college located in Raleigh, NC. The college was founded in 1867 in Raleigh, NC, by prominent Episcopal clergy. Located ten blocks east of the state capitol, Saint Augustine's College is an outgrowth of Christian missionary work by Northerners in the Reconstruction Era, South. It established Raleigh as an educational center or opportunity for freedmen and has graduated, over the years, *many* of the region's most accomplished African Americans. Saint Augustine's, affiliated with the Episcopal Church, began as a normal school with a technical and trade-related program and subsequently adopted a liberal arts curriculum. The name changed to Saint Augustine's School in 1893 and to Saint Augustine's Junior College in 1919. The school became a four-year institution in 1928 and was renamed as Saint Augustine's College. It became St. Augustine's University in 2012.

Relevant Information

Established: 1867

Type: Private, HBCU

Location: 1315 Oakwood Ave., Raleigh, NC 27610

Phone: 919-151-6400

Religious Affiliation: Episcopal Church

Student Enrollment: 1,500

Tuition Fees: $17,160

Academic Staff: NA

Campus: Urban, 105 acres

School Colors: Blue and white

Mascot/Nickname: Falcon

Athletics/Sports Affiliation: NCAA Div. II, CIAA

Endowment: $23 million

Notable Alumni

Bernard Allen: educator and longtime lobbyist for N C Association of Educators and NC House Member.

Hannah D. Atkins: first African American women elected to the Oklahoma House of Representatives.

Luther Barns: gospel music recording artist.

Ralph Campbell Jr.: former North Carolina state auditor.

Travis Cherry: Grammy nominated music producer.

Anna J. Cooper: writer and educator.

Bessie and Sadie Delany: African Americans who published their best-selling memoir *Having Our Say* at ages of 102 and 104, respectively.

Henry B. Delany: first African American Episcopal bishop.

Ruby B. DeMesme: former assistant *secretary* of the air force

Ramon Gittens: Olympics sprinter.

Robert Golphin: actor.

Trevor Graham: former track and head coach.

Alex Hall: former NFL linebacker for Philadelphia Eagles, Arizona

Cardinals, New York Giants, and Canadian Football League.

Ike Lassiter: first NFL player ever from Saint Augustine's College.

William McBran: Medal of Honor recipient.

Angelique Monet: former Miss Black South Carolina.

Hon. James E. C. Perry: justice of Supreme Court of Florida.

Antonio Pettigrew: won Olympic gold medal in men's 4 × 400 meter relay for United States.

ST. PHILIP'S COLLEGE

History

St. Philip's College is a public community college located in San Antonio, TX. St. Philip's, a part of the Alamo Community College District, serves more than 9,000 students in over 70 different academic and technical disciplines. It is the only college to be federally designated as both a historically black college and a Hispanic-serving institution. St. Philips under St. Philips Episcopal Church founded St. Philips Normal and Industrial School to educate and train recently emancipated slaves. In 1902, Artemisia Bowden, daughter of a former slave, joined the school as administrator and teacher, serving for 52 years. In 1942, the school, retaining the St. Philips Junior College name, affiliated- with San Antonio and the San Antonio Independent School District and renamed itself as St. Philip's College.

Relevant Information

Established: 1898

Type: Public, HBCU, and Hispanic

Location: 1801 Martin Luther King Dr., San Antonia, TX 78203

Phone: 210-486-2000

Religious Affiliation: NA

Student Enrollment: 10,313

Tuition Fees: In-state $3,632; out-of-state, $6,420

Academic Staff: NA

Campus: Urban, 600 acres

School Colors: Blue and white

Mascot/Nickname: Tigers

Athletics/Sports Affiliation: NA

Endowment: NA

Notable Alumni

Anthony E. Pratt: inventor of the board game Cluedo.

Don Maclean: entertainer and presenter of Cracker Jack.

Eamon Duffy: professor of the History of Christianity at the University of Cambridge.

John Jenkins: ambassador to Iraq since 2009.

Terrence Rigby: actor.

J. R. R. Tolkien: won Foundation Scholarship to King Edward's School.

Patrick Gallaher CBC: chairman of North West Gas and of Wales Gas Board and president of the Igase.

Paul Leighton: broadcaster and BBC radio 2 newsreader.

Sir Francis Griffin: director of the NEC.

Peter Latham: squadron leader and later air Marshall and station commander of RAF Tengah.

William Slim: served as British commander in chief in Southeast Asia during World War II.

STILLMAN COLLEGE

History

Stillman College is a historically black, liberal arts college founded in 1876. It is located in the West Tuscaloosa area of Tuscaloosa, AL. The college is located on a 105-acre campus and was authorized by the General Assembly of the Presbyterian Church in the United States in 1875. At that time, the name was changed from Tuscaloosa Institute to Stillman Institute. The institute concept was initiated by the Rev. Dr. Charles A. Stillman, pastor of first Presbyterian Church of Tuscaloosa, for training the colored men for the ministry. During 1948-1965, the school sought to expand into a senior liberal arts institution, and in 1948, the name was officially changed to Stillman College. The following year, the school expanded into a four-year college and graduated its first baccalaureate class in 1951. Dr. Harold N. Stinson was the first African American to assume the presidency.

Relevant Information

Established: 1876

Type: Private, HBCU

Location: PO Box 1430, 3600 Stillman Blvd., Tuscaloosa, AL 35403

Phone: 205-349-4240

Religious Affiliation: Presbyterian Church, USA

Student Enrollment: 1,500

Tuition Fees: $7,056

Academic Staff: NA

Campus: Urban, 105 acres

School Colors: Navy blue and gold

Mascot/Nickname: Tigers

Athletics/Sports Affiliation: NCAA Div. ll, SIAC

Endowment: $18,209,397

Notable Alumni

Eddie R. Johnson: deputy state superintendent of education and serves on board of trustees at Stillman.

Teddy Keaton: head football coach at Stillman College.

Junior Galette: NFL end/linebacker; signed with New Orleans Saints.

Sammie L. Hill: defensive back with Detroit Lions.

Quim Porter: running back who played for Green Bay Packers, Cleveland Browns, and St. Louis Rams.

Brian Witherspoon: NFL cornerback with the Jacksonville Jaguars, Detroit Lions, and New York Giants.

TALLADEGA COLLEGE

History

Talladega College—located in Talladega, AL—is a private, liberal arts college. It is the oldest private, historically black college. The history of Talladega College began in 1865 when two former slaves, William Savery and Thomas Tarrant, met at convention with a group of new freedmen in Mobile, AL. As a pledge, Savery and Tarrant, aided by General W. Swayne of the Freedmen's bureau, began to provide a school for the children of former slaves. Meanwhile, the nearby Baptist Academy was about to be sold under mortgage default. This building had been built from 1852 to 1853 with the help of slaves. A speedup plea was sent to General Swayne for its purchase. General Swaney in turn persuaded the AMA to buy the building and some 20 acres of land for $23,000. The grateful parents renamed the building Swayne School, and it was opened in 1867. In 1869, Swayne was issued a charter as Talladega College by the judge of Probate of Talladega County.

Relevant Information

Established: 1887

Type: Private, HBCU

Location: 627 Battle St West, Talladega, AL 35160

Phone: 256-362-0206

Religious Affiliation: United Church of Christ

Student Enrollment: 600

Tuition Fees: $11,492

Academic Staff: 35

Campus: Rural, 50 acres

School Colors: Crimson and blue

Mascot/Nickname: Tornadoes

Athletics/Sports affiliation: NAIA Div. II, GCAC

Endowment: $4,551,651

Notable Alumni

William R. Harvey: current president of Hampton University.

Jewel P. Cobb: biologist and cancer researcher, college dean of California State University.

Nikki Fim: author who won National Book Award for poetry.

Theodore K. Lawless: dermatologist, medical researcher, and philanthropist.

Wynonia Lipman: first African American woman elected to the New Jersey Senate.

Lee Pitts: world renowned swim instructor.

Arthur Shores: civil rights attorney.

Hank Sanders: civil rights attorney and Alabama state senator.

TENNESSEE STATE UNIVERSITY

History

Tennessee State University (TSU) is a land-grant university located in Nashville, TN. TSU is the only state-funded historically black university in Tennessee. The university is a member-school of the Thurgood Marshall College Fund. TSU was originally organized as the Agricultural and Industrial State Normal School in 1909 and began serving students in 1912.

It was elevated to university status in 1951, renamed the Tennessee Agricultural and Industrial University, got full-fledged land-grant university status since 1958. In 1968, the state legislature dropped the words "Agricultural and Industrial" in favor of "TSU." TSU has grown dramatically from a small college to two campuses: the 500-acre main campus and the downtown Avon Williams campus. The diverse student population of 9,000 students represents forty-six states and forty-five countries. TSU offers forty-five bachelor's degrees and twenty-four master's degrees. Doctoral programs include biological sciences, psychology, public administration, computer information systems, and engineering administration.

Relevant Information

Established: 1912

Type: Public, HBCU

Location: 3500 John Merritt Blvd., Nashville, TN 37209

Phone: 615-963-5000

Religious Affiliation: NA

Student Enrollment: 8,456

Tuition Fees: Out-of-state $18,616

Academic Staff: 573

Campus: Urban, 903 acres

School Colors: Blue and white

Mascot/Nickname: Tigers

Athletics/sports affiliation: NCAA and Ohio Valley Conference

Endowment: $28.8 million

Notable Alumni

Brent Alexander: NFL football player.

Bennie Anderson: NFL football player.

Dick Barnett: NBA basketball player.

Jimmy Blanton: jazz musician.

Ralph Boston: won in Olympic long jump three times.

Waymond Bryant: NFL football player.

Greg Carr: chair of the Department of Afro-American Studies, Howard University.

Chandra Cheeseborough: Olympic runner; gold and silver medal winner.

Hank Crawford: jazz musician.

Dave Davis: NFL football player.

Richard Dent: NFL football player and member of Pro Football Hall of Fame.

Lamar Divens: NFL football player.

Larry Tharpe: NFL football player.

Cleveland Eaton: jazz musician.

Cleveland Elam: NFL football player.

Charley Ferguson: AFL football player.

Sean Foley: golf instructor to PGA Tour players.

Ryan Fann: Paralympics runner.

Harold Ford: member of the US Congress.

John Ford: member of Tennessee Senate.

Randy Fuller: NFL football player.

Howard Gentry: politician.

Joe Gilliam: NFL football player.

W. C. Gorden: former head football coach at Jackson State University and member of College Football Hall of Fame.

Moses Gunn: actor.

Thelma Harper: member of Tennessee Senate.

Mike Hegman: NFL football player.

Claude Humphrey: NFL football player.

Daniel Johnson: NFL football player.

Harvey Johnson, Jr.: mayor of Jackson.

Joe Johnson: jazz musician.

Ed "Too Tall" Jones: NFL football player

Joe "Turkey" Jones: NFL football player.

Larry Kinnebrew: NFL football player.

Anthony Levine: NFL football player.

Madeline Manning: Olympic runner; gold medalist.

Anthony Mason: NBA basketball player.

Edith McGuire: Olympic runner; gold and two silver medalists.

Steve Moore: NFL football player.

Samuel G. Puryear: Queens University director of Golf Operations and head of the Professional Golf Management Program.

Lloyd Neal: NBA basketball player.

Leonard "Truck" Robinson: NBA basketball player.

Dominique R- Cromartie: NFL football player.

Carlos Rogers: former NBA basketball player.

Carl Rowan: journalist.

Wilma Rudolph: Olympic runner; first women to win three gold medals in a single Olympics.

Simon Shanks: NFL football player.

Nate Simpson: NFL football player.

Ollie Smith: NFL football player.

Carla Thomas: singer.

Leon Thomas: jazz singer.

Rufus Thomas: singer.

Wyomia Tyus: Olympic runner; first person to retain the Olympic title in the 100 meters.

Tina Tyus-Shaw: reporter.

Charlie Wade: NFL football player.

Carl Water: NFL football player.

A C Wharton: mayor of Memphis, Tennessee.

Javarris Williams: NFL football player.

Oprah Winfrey: talk show host, actress, entrepreneur.

Samuel Vette: journalist, author, and educator.

TEXAS COLLEGE

History

Texas College is a historically black, four-year college located in Tyler, TX that is affiliated with the Christian Methodist Episcopal (CME) Church and the UNCF. The school was established by CME ministers in 1894 and briefly changed its name to Phillips University from 1909 to 1912. Texas College offers bachelor's degree programs in arts, biology, business administration, computer science, English, education, history, mathematics, music, physical education, political science, liberal studies, social work, and sociology. Also available are associate of arts degrees in early childhood education and general studies, as well as an alternative certification teacher education program for people with bachelor's degrees.

Relevant Information

Established: 1894

Type: Private, HBCU

Location: 2404 Grand Ave., Tyler, TX 75702

Phone: 903-593-8311

Religious Affiliation: CME Church

Student Enrollment: 600

Tuition Fees: Off campus $16,682; on campus $9,682

Academic Staff: NA

Campus: Urban, 25 *acres*

School Colors: Purple and gold

Mascot/Nickname: Steers

Athletics/Sports Affiliation: NAIA, RRAC, CSFL

Endowment: $1.6 million

TEXAS SOUTHERN UNIVERSITY

History

Texas Southern University, shortened as Texas Southern or TSU, is a historically black university (HBCU) located in Houston, TX, and accredited by the SACS. The university was established in 1927 as the Houston Colored Junior College through its private college phase as Houston Colored College. In 1947, the state declared this to be the first state university in Houston, and it was renamed Texas State University for Negroes. In 1951, the name was changed to TSU. Texas Southern is one of the largest and most comprehensive HBCUs in the nation and one of only four independent public universities in Texas. TSU is the only HBCU in Texas recognized as one of America's Top Colleges by *Forbes*. TSU is recognized as the leading producers of college degrees to African Americans and Hispanics in Texas and ranks fourth in the nation in African American conferred doctoral and professional degrees. The university is a member of the Thurgood Marshall College Fund.

Relevant Information

Established: 1927

Type: Public, HUBC

243

Location: 3100 Cleburne St., Houston, TX 77004

Phone: 713-313-7011

Religious Affiliation: Independent

Student Enrollment: 10,026

Tuition Fees: $34,229

Academic Staff: Faculty

Campus: Urban, 150 acres

School Colors: Gray and maroon

Mascot/Nickname: Tigers

Athletics/Sports Affiliation: NCAA Div. I, SWAC

Endowment: $35,415,720

Notable Alumni

Barbara C. Jordan: Congresswoman in the US House of Representatives.

Mickey Leland: antipoverty activist and later chair of the Congressional Black caucus.

Doris H. Pemberton: civic leader, reporter, and author.

Yolanda Adams: American Grammy and Dove Award winner, gospel singer, and radio host.

Michael Strahan: former NFL defensive end for New York Giants and currently football analyst on Fox News Sunday.

Kirk Whalum: jazz saxophonist.

Rocky Williform: American entrepreneur and founder of Hip-Hop Blog and was named one of the most influential people in hip-hop culture.

Harry E. Johnson: current president of Washington, D.C., Martin L. King, Jr. National Memorial Project Foundation.

Ronald C. Green: current city controller of Houston.

Rodney Ellis: member of Texas Senate.

Jarvis Johnson: member of the Houston City Council.

Kase Lukman: chairman and chief executive officer of CAMAC.

Sentronia Thompson: member of the Texas House of Representatives.

Lloyd C. Wells: sports photographer and civil rights activist.

Robert Taylor: Olympics gold medalist in 4 × 100 m relay and in 4 × 400 m relay.

Ken Burrough: former NFL wide receiver.

DeJuan Fulghum: current NFL linebacker.

Brett Maxie: former NFL defensive back.

Lloyd Mumphord: former NFL defensive back.

Julius Adams: former NFL defensive lineman.

Cortez Hankton: former NFL wide receiver.

Oliver Celestin: former NFL defensive back.

Don Narcisse: former CFL wide receiver.

Warren Bone: former NFL player.

Belvin Perry: chief judge of Ninth Judicial Circuit in Orlando, FL.

Jim Hines: winner of two gold medals in Olympics.

TOUGALOO COLLEGE

History

Tougaloo College is a private, co-educational, historically black, liberal arts institution of higher education founded in 1869 in Madison County, north of Jackson, MS. Originally established by New York-based Christian missionaries for the education of freed slaves and their offspring, from 1871 until 1892 the college served as a teacher training school by the State of Mississippi. In 1869, the American Missionary Association (AMA) of New York purchased 500 acres of one of the largest former plantations in Mississippi to build a college for freedmen and their children. The state granted the new institution a formal charter under the name of Tougaloo University. Six years after Tougaloo's founding, the Home Missionary Society of the Christian Church (Disciples of Christ) obtained a charter to establish a school at Edwards, MS, to be known as Southern Christian Institute. In 1962, with the agreement of both supporting bodies, the school's name was returned to its last 1954 merger, Tougaloo College.

Relevant information

Established: 1869

Type: Private, HBCU

Location: 500 West County Line Rd., Tougaloo, MS 39174

Phone: 601-197-7700

Religious Affiliation: United Church of Christ

Student Enrollment: 900

Tuition Fees: $17,025

Academic Staff: 100

Campus: Suburban, 500 acres

School Colors: Royal blue and scarlet

Mascot/Nickname: Bulldogs

Athletics/Sports Affiliation: NAIA, GCAC

Endowment: $9,370,847

Notable Alumni

Colia Clark: civil rights activist.

Aunjanue Ellis: actor.

Lawrence Guyot: civil rights activist and director of Mississippi Freedom Democratic Party.

Joyce Ladner: sociologist, civil rights activist, and first female president of Howard University.

Anne Moody: author and civil rights activist.

Aaron Shirley: founder of Jackson Medical Mall and recipient of MacArthur

Award.

Bennie Thompson: US Congressman.

Walter Turnbull: founder of the Boys' Choir of Harlem.

Walter Washington: past president of Alcorn State University and past president of Alpha Phi Alpha Fraternity.

H. COUNCILL TRENHOLM STATE TECHNICAL COLLEGE

History

H. Councill Trenholm State Technical College was created through merging John M. Patterson State Technical College with H. Councill Trenholm State Technical College. On April 27, 2000, the Alabama State Board of Education, upon recommendation of the chancellor of Postsecondary Education, approved the intent to merge. Since both colleges were technical colleges, the merger did not alter that status or result in *any* change in the role of the new entity. On April 2001, the Alabama State Board of Education voted to name the newly created entity H. Councill Trenholm State Technical College. The college maintains two campuses: the Patterson Campus and the Trenholm Campus, which are only 8.9 miles apart.

Relevant Information

Established: 1963

Type: Public, two-year college

Location: 1225 Air Base Bid. Montgomery, AIL 36108

Phone: 334-420-4200

Religious Affiliation: NA

Student Enrollment: 4,999

Tuition Fees: In-state, $2,784; out-of-state $5,568

Academic Staff: 134

Campus: Urban, Patterson (43 acres); Trenholm (25 acres)

School Colors: NA

Mascot/Nickname: HBCU Connect

Athletic/Sports Affiliation: HBCU Connect

Endowment: NA

Notable Alumni

NA

TUSKEGEE UNIVERSITY

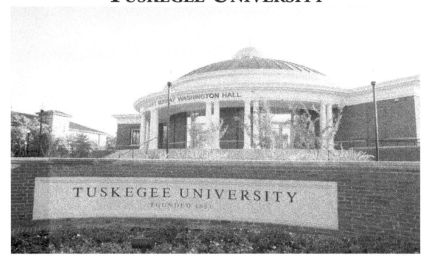

History

Tuskegee University is a private, historically black university located in Tuskegee, AL, established by Booker T. Washington. The university is the home to over 3,000 students from the United States and 30 foreign countries. The campus has been designated as the Tuskegee Institute National Historical Site, a National Historical Landmark. Tuskegee University is the only HBCU to hold this distinction. It is the home of the famed Tuskegee Airmen, scientist George Washington Carver, and Architect Robert R. Taylor. The university offers thirty-five bachelor's degree programs, twelve master's degree programs, a five-year accredited professional degree program in architecture, two doctoral degree programs, and the Doctor of Veterinary Medicine. It is the only HBCU to offer the Doctor of Veterinary Medicine.

Relevant Information

Established: 1881

Type: Private, HBCU

Location: 1200 W Montgomery Rd., Tuskegee, AL 36088

Phone: 334-172-7801

Religious Affiliation: NA

Student Enrollment: 3,156

Tuition Fees: In-state and out-of-state $27,102

Academic Staff: NA

Campus: Rural, 5,000 acres

School Colors: Old gold and crimson

Mascot/Nickname: Tigers

Athletics/Sports Affiliation: SACS

Endowment: $105 million

Notable Alumni

Amelia B. Robinson: international civil and human rights activist.

Robert Beck: writer.

Charles W. Carpenter: Baptist minister and civil rights activist.

Alice M. Coachman: American athlete and Olympic gold medal winner.

The Commodores: 70s R&B band that met while attending.

Tuskegee George W. Crawford: lawyer and city official in New Haven, CT.

Leon Crenshaw: former NFL player.

Oliver W. Dillard: retired army major general, Silver Star recipient.

Ralph Ellison: scholar and author of *Invisible Man*.

Milton Davis: lawyer involved in famous Scottsboro Case.

Vera K. Farris: president of Richard Stockton College of New Jersey.

Drayton Florence: current NFL defensive back.

Isaac Rsher: educator.

Mack C. Gaston: Admiral in US Navy, commanded two ships.

Alexander N. Green: US Representative from Texas.

Marvalene Hughes: president of Dillard University.

Daniel "Chappie" James: first African American US Air Force pilot to reach the rank of four-star general.

Lonnie Johnson: inventor.

Ken Jordan: former NFL player.

Tom Joyner: American radio host whose daily program is *The Tom Joyner Morning Show.*

John A. Lankford: twentieth-century architect.

Marion Mann: former dean of College of Medicine at Howard University.

Claude McKay: Jamaican writer and poet.

Leo Morton: chancellor of the University of Missouri, Kansas City.

Albert Murray: literary and jazz critic, novelist, and biographer.

Ray Nagin: former mayor of New Orleans.

Gertrude Nelson: military, civilian, and American Red Cross nurse and college administrator.

Dimitri Patterson: current NFL player.

Dorothy Richey: first woman to be appointed as the head of athletics at Chicago State University.

Ptolemy A. Reid: prime minister of Guyana, 1980-1984. Lionel Richie: R&B singer, Grammy Award winner.

UNIVERSITY OF THE VIRGIN ISLANDS

History

The University of the Virgin Islands (or UVI) is a public university located in the US Virgin Islands. The university is a member-school of the Thurgood Marshall College Fund. UVI is accredited by the Commission on Higher Education of the Middle States Association of Colleges and Schools. The school was founded in 1962. It officially became one of the HBCUs in 1986 and offers undergraduate and graduate degree programs in business, education, liberal arts, nursing, and mathematics. The university has strong academic programs under its College of Science and Mathematics and an early medical school and selection program with Boston University, which affords selected students to study for three years at UVI and then transfer to Boston University Medical School in their senior year.

Relevant Information

Established: 1962

Type: Public, HBCU

Location: Charlotte Amalie West, St. Thomas, US Virgin Islands

Phone: 340-776-9200

Religious Affiliation: NA

Student Enrollment: 2,392

Tuition Fees: In-state $19,474; out-of-state $27,854

Academic Staff: 107

Campus: Urban, acreage: NA

School Colors: White and blue

Mascot/Nickname: Buccaneers

Athletics/Sports Affiliation: NCAA, CUSA

Endowment: NA

Notable Alumni

Granville Wrensford: former chair of Albany State University's Department of Natural Sciences.

Richard Skerritt: UVI's first-ever Rhodes Scholar, businessman, and manager of West Indies cricket team.

VIRGINIA STATE UNIVERSITY

History

Virginia State University is a historically black, land-grant university located north of the Appomattox River in Ettrick, Chesterfield County, near Petersburg, VA. Founded in March 1882, Virginia State University developed as the United States' first fully state-supported four-year institution of higher learning for black Americans. The university is a member of the Thurgood Marshall College Fund. In 1902, the legislature revised the school's charter and renamed it the Virginia Normal and Industrial Institute. In 1923, the college was renamed Virginia State College for Negroes, shortened to Virginia State College in 1946. In 1979, the institution's addition of more departments and graduate programs was recognized in a change to Virginia State University. Meanwhile, the school's two-year branch in Norfolk, VA, founded in 1935, was expanded to a four-year curriculum and renamed Norfolk State College, which was later renamed to NSU.

Relevant Information

Established: 1882

Type: Public, HBCU

Location: 1 Stewart St., Petersburg, VA 23806

Phone: 757-524-5000

Religious Affiliation: NA

Student Enrollment: 6,000

Tuition Fees: In-state $7,090; out-of-state $15,458

Academic Staff: NA

Campus: Suburban, 236 acres

School Colors: Orange and blue

Mascot/Nickname: Trojans

Athletics/Sports Affiliation: NCAA Div. I, CIAA

Endowment: $13.6 million

Notable Alumni

Gaye Adegbalola: blues singer and civil rights activist.

James Avery: actor.

Joe Bonner: jazz pianist.

Herman Branson: African American physicist.

Rovenia M. Brock: nutritionist, lecturer, health reporter, author, and entrepreneur.

AI Bumbry: Major League baseball player.

Larry Brooks: former NFL defensive lineman for Los Angeles Rams.

James Brown: former NFL player.

Pamela E. Bridgewater: former US Ambassador to Ghana and current ambassador to Jamaica.

Myles "Ray" Cunningham: cast member of Bets *College Hill* series.

Rosalyn Dance: politician and member of Virginia House of Delegates.

Das EFX: rap group.

Silas DeMary: Arena Football League player.

Wale Folarin: rapper from Washington, D.C.

Robert L Gregory: judge, US Court of Appeals.

Aaron Hall: member of the music group Guy.

Damian Hall: member of the music group Guy.

Delores G. Kelly: member of the Maryland State Senate.

Reginald Lewis: businessman and owner of TLC Beatrice International.

William H. Lewis: former US Assistant Attorney General.

Naomi L. Madgett: teacher and award-winning poet, editor of Lotus Press.

Thomas Miller: prolific graphic designer and visual artist.

Hector M. Munoz: first member of Supreme Court of Puerto Rico.

James H. Stith: African American physicist and Professor of Physics at Ohio State University.

Roslyn Tyler: politician and member of Virginia House of Delegates.

Billy Taylor: jazz musician.

Camilla Williams: first African American to receive a contract from a major opera company.

Avis Wyatt: professional basketball player.

Ronica Wynder: television producer and fiction author.

Anthony L. Burfoot: vice mayor of the City of Norfolk.

VIRGINIA UNION UNIVERSITY

History

Virginia Union University is a historically black university located in Richmond, VA. It took its present name in 1899 upon the merger of two older schools, Richmond Theological and Wayland Seminary, each founded after the end of the American Civil War by the American Baptist Home Mission Society. Its *84-acre* campus is located at 1500 North Lombardy Street in Richmond's North Side. Virginia Union University was founded in 1865 to give the newly emancipated freedmen an opportunity for education of the mind in an ethical, religious environment. The university seeks to empower students for the pursuit of lifelong learning in providing comprehensive undergraduate liberal arts programs and graduate education for Christian ministries. To this end, a guiding principle of the university's education is a strong focus upon moral values and ethics, and students are encouraged in activities that promote self-actualization. The American Baptist Home Mission Society founded the school in 1865, and a "National Theological Institute" to educate freedmen wishing to enter the Baptist ministry. This effort was the beginning of *Virginia* Union University. Separate branches of the NTI were set up in Washington, D.C. The branches became known as Wayland Seminary. In 1899, the Richmond Theological Institute joined with Wayland Seminary to form the Virginia Union University in Richmond, VA.

Relevant Information

Established: 1865

Type: Private, HBCU

Location: 1500 North Lombardy St., Richmond, VA 23220

Phone: 804-257-5600

Religious Affiliation: American Baptist

Student Enrollment: 1,700

Tuition Fees: $14,630

Academic Staff: NA

Campus: Urban, 84 *acres*

School Colors: Maroon and steel

Mascot/Nickname: Panthers

Athletics/Sports Affiliation: NCAA Div. II, CIAA

Endowment: $29 million

Notable Alumni

James Atkins: former NFL player.

Mamye BaCote: member of Virginia House of Delegates.

Bessye J. Bearden: journalist and social activist.

Michael Brim: award-winning journalist and first African American reporter for the *Washington Post.*

Roslyn M. Brock: chair of NAACP.

Henry A. Bullock: historian and winner of Bancroft Prize.

Emmett C. Bums: member of Maryland House of Delegates.

Terry Davis: former NBA player.

Robert P. Daniel: former president of Shaw and Virginia State Universities.

Will Downing: R&B singer.

A. J. English: professional basketball player.

Walter Fauntroy: civil rights leader, minister and former member of the US House of Representatives in Washington, D.C.

Anderson J. Franklin: professor of psychology at Boston College.

Samuel L. Gravely: first African American to reach the rank of admiral in US Navy.

Abram L. Harris: economist, chair of Economics Department, Howard University.

Pete Hunter: NFL league player.

Eugene K. Jones: member of black cabinet under President Franklin D. Roosevelt.

Dwight c. Jones: mayor of Richmond, VA.

Howard S. Jones: inventor, microwave systems hardware.

Charles S. Johnson: first black president of Fisk University.

Lyman T. Johnson: integrated the University of Kentucky.

Leontine T. Kelly: bishop of United Methodist Church.

Henry Marsh: first African American mayor of Richmond, VA.

Bai T. Moore: Liberian author and poet.

Deloris McQuinn: member of Virginia House of Delegates.

Charles Oakley: NBA basketball player.

Chandler Owen: writer, editor, and early member of the Socialist Party.

Wendell H. Phillips: member of Maryland House of Delegates.

Samuel D. Proctor: president of Virginia Union and A&T State Universities.

John W. Kinney: dean at Samuel DeWitt Proctor School of Theology at Virginia Union University.

Randall Robinson: attorney and founder of TransAfrica.

James A. Roebuck: member of Pennsylvania House of Representatives.

Spottswood W. Robinson, Ill: prominent civil rights attorney and first

African American appointed to US District Court.

Herbert Scott: NFL player, All-Pro, Dallas Cowboys.

Wyatt T. Walker: activist, civil rights motivational speaker, musician, theologian, and close confidant of Martin L. King.

Ben Wallace: NBA defensive player, NBA champions, Detroit Pistons.

Douglas Wilder: first African American Governor of Virginia and mayor of Richmond, VA.

Donald F. Turner: professor at Harvard Law School.

VIRGINIA UNIVERSITY OF LYNCHBURG

History

Virginia University of Lynchburg is a private, historically black university located in Lynchburg, VA. The university currently offers instruction and degrees, primarily in religious studies, including a doctorate of ministry program. Virginia University of Lynchburg is the oldest school of higher learning in Lynchburg, VA. The school was founded in 1886 and incorporated in 1888 by the Virginia Baptist State Convention as the coeducational "Lynchburg Baptist Seminary." Classes were first held in 1890 under the name Virginia Seminary. *With* the offering of a collegiate program in 1900, the name was again changed to Virginia Theological Seminary and College. In 1962, the institution was renamed to the Virginia Seminary and College. In 1996, the school was given its current name.

Relevant Information

Established: 1886

Type: Private, HBCU

Location: 2058 Garfield Ave., Lynchburg, VA 24501

Phone: 434-152-5276

Religious Affiliation: Virginia Baptist State Convention

Student Enrollment: 600

Tuition Fees: $17,406

Academic Staff: NA

Campus: Suburban, acreage: NA

School Colors: Gray and crimson

Mascot/Nickname: Dragons

Athletics/Sports Affiliation: USCAA

Endowment: NA

Notable Alumni

NA

VOORHEES COLLEGE

History

Voorhees College is a private, historically black college (HBCU) in Denmark, SC. It is affiliated with the Episcopal Church. The college is accredited by the Southern Association of Colleges and Schools (SACS). In 1897, Elizabeth E. Wright and Jessie Dorsey founded Denmark Industrial School for African Americans. Located in a rural area and small town, it was modeled on Tuskegee Institute. In 1902, Ralph Voorhees, a New Jersey philanthropist, gave the school a donation to purchase land and construct buildings. In 1904, the South Carolina General Assembly renamed the school and incorporated it as the Voorhees Industrial Institute for Colored Youths. In 1947, its name was changed to Voorhees School and Junior College. In 1962, with the addition of departments, it became accredited as Voorhees College. After the students protested for more black study programs and for hiring more black faculty, the president of Voorhees agreed to the students' demands.

Relevant Information

Established: 1897

Type: Private, HBCU

Location: 481 Porter Dr., Denmark, SC 29042

Phone: 803-780-1180

Religious Affiliation: Episcopal Church

Student Enrollment: 600

Tuition Fees: $10,780

Academic Staff: NA

Campus: Rural, 350 acres

School Colors: Royal blue and white

Mascot/Nickname: Tigers

Athletics/Sports Affiliation: NAIA and ALL

Endowment: NA

Notable Alumni

Dannon Lindley: grants/budgets analyst for US Department of Labor/ Employment and Training Administration.

Sarah Simpson: served as second vice president of the college's National Alumni Association.

Kevin Crosby: named first African American head football coach for Bamberg-Ehrhardt High School.

Tamara S. Webster: one of the seven dentists working with the group called Danville Dental Associates in Danville, VA.

Mike Gagum: senior vice president of Concentrix.

Tywana Branch: received the SCICU Teaching Award.

Ronnie A. Sabb: president and executive officer of the law offices of Ronnie A Sabb, LLC.

Alfonzo Williams: first African American chief of the Waynesboro Police Department, GA.

Patrick A. Williamson: self-published his first book, *Growing in Grace: Wisdom for Empowered Living*.

David Miller: cofounder of *Our Weekly* group of newspapers in Los Angeles.

Ronald Williams: an academic specialist in the US Department of Education's Upward Bound Program.

Nate Robinson: serves as deputy director for the Defense Logistics Agency in Battle Creek, MI.

Jim Reaves: served as researcher for the USDA Forest Service.

Tywana Branch: professor of Psychology at Voorhees College & S.C. Independent Colleges Awardee.

Ken Griffin: a member of the Charlotte 49ers coaching staff.

Pamela M. Wilson: twenty-fourth president of Allen University.

Dianna Richburg: received 2010 Teacher of the Year Award at Denmark Olar Elementary School.

Garon Jackson: head cross country and distant coach at Voorhees College and Bethune-Cookman University.

Captain Brittiane Staton: awards include Army Commendation Medal, National Defense Service Medal, Global War on Terrorism Service Medal, German Armed Forces Badge, Korean Service Ribbon, and Army Service Ribbon.

Benjamin Watson: currently serving as the assistant director of admissions at the Citadel.

Shampal Williams: had the story "Left Behind" in the book, *Souls of My Young Sisters*.

Dameone Ferguson: employed with the Department of Defense, where he oversee grants and internships for minority for the NNSA.

Javon Jackson: was hired for the GE Appliances and Lighting Plant Financial Leadership program.

WEST VIRGINIA STATE UNIVERSITY

History

West Virginia State University is a historically black, public college in Institute, West Virginia located in the Charleston-metro area. The school is usually referred to as State or West Virginia State. It is one of the original 1890 land-grant colleges and the smallest land-grant institution in the country. The university is a member of the Thurgood Marshall College Fund. The school was established as the West Virginia Colored Institute in 1891 under the Morrill Act, which provided land-grant institutions for black students in the seventeen states that had segregated schools. Booker T. Washington, noted African American educator and statesman, was instrumental in having the institution located in the Kanawha Valley. Dr. Washington visited the campus often and spoke at its first commencement exercise. Renamed in 1915 as West Virginia Collegiate Institute, it became West Virginia State College in 1929. In 1954, following the Brown Decision to desegregate public education, the institution transformed from an all-black college with a primarily residential population to a predominantly commuter school with mostly white students. Between 2011-2012 the school's population was 61% white and 12.5% black.

Relevant Information

Established: 1891

Type: Public, HBCU

Location: 5000 Fairlawn Ave., Dunbar, WV 25112

Phone: 304-176-6000

Religious Affiliation: NA

Student Enrollment: 2,644

Tuition Fees: $4,918

Academic Staff: NA

Campus: suburban, 91 acres

School Colors: Black and gold

Mascot/Nickname: "State" or "West Virginia State" also "Yellow Jackets"

Athletics/Sports Affiliation: NCAA Div. II, WVAlAC

Endowment: $3.2 million

Notable Alumni

Katherine Johnson: African American scientist who had made significant contributions to America's aeronautics and space for NASA.

Chu Berry: jazz tenor saxophonist.

Antoine Fuqua: writer and director of various movies.

Earl Lloyd: first African American to play in the NBA.

Lou Myers: actor and theatrical director, played as Vernon Gaines in *A Different World.*

Will Robinson: first African American Div. I basketball coach and NFL scout.

Leon Sullivan: Baptist minister, civil rights leader and activist, and board member for General Motors longtime.

Butch Miles: jazz drummer and professor in the School of Music at Texas State University, San Marcos.

Harriet E. Byrd: first African American to serve in the Wyoming Legislature.

WILBERFORCE UNIVERSITY

History

Wilberforce University is a private, coed, liberal arts, historically black college and university (HBCU) located in Wilberforce, OH. Affiliated with the African Methodist Episcopal (AME) Church, it was the first college to be owned and operated by African Americans. It participates in the United Negro College Fund (UNCF).

The founding of the college was unique as a collaboration in 1856 by the Cincinnati, Ohio Conference of the Methodist Episcopal Church and the AME Church. They planned a college to provide classical education and teacher training for black youth. When the number of students fell due to American Civil War and financial losses, the college was closed. In 1863, the AME church purchased the institution to ensure its survival. The college attracted the top professors of the day, including W. E. Dubois. In the nineteenth century, it enlarged its mission to include students from South Africa. The university supports the National Association of African American Museum to broaden the reach of its programs and assist smaller museums with professional standards.

Relevant Information

Established: 1856

Type: Private, HBCU

Location: 1055 North Bickett Rd., Wilberforce, OH 45384

Phone: 937-376-2911

Religious Affiliation: AME

Student Enrollment: 489

Tuition Fees: In-state and out-of-state $21,670

Academic Staff: NA

Campus: Rural, 125 acres

School Colors: Green and gold

Mascot/Nickname: Bulldogs

Athletics/Sports Affiliation: NAIA, AMC

Endowment: $50 million+

Notable Alumni

Victoria Gray Adams: pioneering civil rights activist.

Regina M. Anderson: playwright librarian, member of the Harlem Renaissance.

Helen Elsie Austin: US Foreign Service Officer.

Myron (Tiny) Bradshaw: American jazz, rhythm and blues bandleader, singer, pianist, and drummer.

Hallie Quinn Brown: educator, writer, and activist.

Charity Adams Earley: first African American woman to be an officer in the Women's Army Auxiliary Corps.

Floyd H. Flake: U.S. Congressman & President of Wilberforce University

Frank Foster: American musician, member of the Count Basie Orchestra.

John R. Fox: recipient of Medal of Honor.

Raymond V. Haysbert: business executive and civil rights leader.

James H. McGee: city commissioner and first African American mayor of Dayton, OH.

Arnett "Ace" Mumford: former football coach at Southern University, Jarvis Christian College, and Bishop College.

Leontyne Price: opera singer and first African American prima donna of the Metropolitan Opera.

George Russell: American jazz composer and theorist.

William G. Still: composer and first African American to conduct a major American Orchestra.

Theophilus G. Steward: US Army chaplain and Buffalo Soldier.

Ossian Sweet: African American doctor notable for self-defense in 1925 against a white mob.

Ben Webster: American jazz musician.

William J. Wilson: American sociologist and Harvard University professor.

Milton Wright: economist.

Mark Wilson: entrepreneur.

WILEY COLLEGE

History

Wiley College is a four-year, private, historically black, liberal arts college, located on the west side of Marshall, TX. Founded in 1873 by the Methodist Episcopal Church's Bishop Isaac Wiley and certified in 1882 by the Freedmen's Aid Society. It is notable as one of the oldest predominant black college west of the Mississippi River. Wiley's mission is to educate students who are prepared for leadership and service when they graduate. Students find that their close interaction with faculty and staff provides for a full and lasting educational experience. Wiley has been ranked as one of the best values among the 320 comprehensive colleges in four regions: North, South, Midwest, and West. It has also been ranked in the western region for highest acceptance rate among comprehensive colleges, offering baccalaureate degrees, as well as having the largest percentage of alumni donors.

Relevant Information

Established: 1873

Type: Private, HBCU

Location: 711 Wiley Ave., Marshall, TX 75670

Phone: 903-927-3300

Religious Affiliation: United Methodist Church

Student Enrollment: 1,200

Tuition Fees: $11,050

Academic Staff: NA Campus: Urban, 134 acres

School Colors: Purple and white

Mascot/Nickname: Wildcats

Athletics/Sports Affiliation: NAIA, RRAC, SWAC Endowment: $50 million

Notable Alumni

R. E. Brown: organized the first male quartet, first brass band, and first football team at Wiley.

Lois Towles: internationally renowned concert pianist.

Henrietta B. Wells: first female member of the debate team at historically black Wiley College.

Thelma Dewitty: first African American to teach in the Seattle Public Schools.

James L. Farmer: US civil rights leader.

Conrad 0. Johnson: music educator.

Henry C. McBay: chemist and college professor.

Bill Spiller: African American golfer who challenged the segregation polices of the PGA.

Heman M. Sweatt: plaintiff in US Supreme Court case "Sweatt v. Painter."

Lee w. Thomas: prominent African American businessman in the oil industry.

James Wheaton: actor, director, and educator.

Jesse J. Williams: chemical engineer and theologian.

Richard Williams: jazz trumpeter.

Floyd Iglehart: NFL player.

George Kinney: NFL player.

Mike Lewis: NFL player.

Lee Thomas: NFL player.

Kelton Winston: NFL player.

WINSTON-SALEM, NORTH CAROLINA

History

Winston-Salem State University (WSSU)—a constituent institution of the University of North Carolina—is a historically black, public, research university in Winston-Salem, NC. It is a member of the Thurgood Marshall College Fund. The town educators of Winston (before it merged in 1913 with Salem to become Winston-Salem) lured Dr. Simon G. Atkins, a distinguished educator, to the post as principal of the Depot Street School, where he remained until 1895. This was the state's largest public school for African Americans. His work with the North Carolina Negro Teachers' Association, which he helped to organize about 1881, had stimulated his interest in teacher training schools for blacks. He directed this group as it established the foundation for a black teachers college in the state. The university was established by Dr. Atkins in 1892 with funds donated by industrialist John F. Slater. It was chartered by the state of North Carolina as Slater Industrial and State Normal School in 1897 and renamed as Winston-Salem Teachers College in 1925. The name was changed to WSSU in 1969, and it merged into the University of North Carolina System in 1972.

Relevant Information

Established: 1892

Type: Public, HBCU

Location: 601 South Martin Luther King Dr., Winston-Salem, NC 21110

Phone: 336-750-2000

Religious Affiliation: NA

Student Enrollment: 6,442

Tuition Fees: In-state $16,038; out-of-state $25,188

Academic Staff: 400

Campus: Urban, 117 acres

School Colors: Red and white

Mascot/Nickname: Rams

Athletics/Sports Affiliation: NCAA Div. II, CIAA

Endowment: $19.6 millions

Notable Alumni

Selma Burke: world renowned artist.

Louis Farrakhan: leader of Nation of Islam.

Earl "The Pearl" Monroe: NBA player and selected as one of its greatest players in league history.

Lorraine H. Morton: mayor of Evanston, IL.

Jim Garner: mayor of Hempstead, NY.

Bias Gilbert: world-class Olympic hurdler.

Stephen A. Smith: sports writer and NBA columnist.

Anthony Blaylock: Atlanta business entrepreneur.

Louise Smith: credited with helping to establish kindergarten program in public schools of North Carolina.

Fredrick Poe: Detroit auto dealer and business entrepreneur.

Joseph D. Johnson: listed as one of the top African American attorneys in the United States.

Donald Bradley: president of the Newark, NJ, City Council.

Larry Womble: representative for the North Carolina Legislature.

Michael P. Decker: representative for the N.C. Legislature

Earline Parmon: representative for N. C. Legislature

Theodore Blunt: president of City Council, Wilmington, DE, 1965.

Walter Marshall: commissioner of Forsyth County, 1965.

Victor Johnson: Forsyth County Board of Education official.

Beaufort Baily: commissioner, 1957.

Yancey Thigpen: former NFL receiver for Tennessee *Titans,* Pittsburg Steelers, and San Diego Chargers.

Oronde Gadsden: NFL wide receiver with Miami Dolphins.

Richard Huntley: NFL running back for Atlanta Falcons, Pittsburg Steelers, Carolina Panthers, and Detroit Lions.

Donald Evans: former NFL player for Los Angeles Rams, Philadelphia Eagles, and Pittsburg Steelers.

Thomas A. Beard Jr.: Corporal Morrell at the John F. Kennedy Center for Performing Arts.

Maria Howell: performing artist.

Joel McIver: published novelist.

Ernest E. Newton: deputy president pro tempore of the Connecticut Senate and chair of Phallic Safety, Hartford, CT.

Cleo Hill: first basketball player from the CIAA to be a first-round draft choice in the NBA.

Xavier University of Louisiana

History

Xavier University of Louisiana—located in the Gert Town section of New Orleans, La. is a private, coeducational, liberal arts college with the distinction of being the only historically black Roman Catholic institution of higher education. Xavier University was established in 1925 when St. Katharine Drexel and the Sisters of the Blessed Sacrament founded the coeducational secondary from which it evolved. Aware of the serious lack of Catholic-oriented education available to young blacks in the South, St. Katharine came to New Orleans and established a high school on the site previously occupied by Southern University. The high school continues on today as Xavier University Preparatory School, known as Xavier Prep. In 1925, Xavier University became a reality when the College of Liberal Arts and Sciences was established. Recognizing the university's need for a separate identity and room to expand, St. Katharine bought a tract of undeveloped land for its present campus.

Relevant Information

Established: 1915

Type: Private, HBCU

Location: 1 Drexel-Dr., New Orleans, LA 70125

Phone: 504-486-7411

Religious Affiliation: Catholic Church, Sisters of the Blessed Sacrament

Tuition Fees: $20,560

Academic Staff: NA

Campus: Urban, 27- acres

Campus Type & Size: Urban, 27 acres

School Colors: Gold and white

Mascot/Nickname: Gold Rush

Athletics/Sports Affiliation: GCAC

Notable Alumni

Nathaniel Clifton: first African American to sign a contract with an NBA team.

Alvin J. Boutte: founder and CEO of Indecorp, the largest black-owned financial institution in the United States.

Ernest N. Morial: first African American mayor of New Orleans and current head of National Urban League.

Bernard P. Randolph: retired USAF general, only the third black to reach the rank of four-star general in any branch.

John Stroger: first African American president of Cook County Board of Commissioners, IL.

Charles Champion: community pharmacist, specialist in the use of herbal medicines.

Marino Casem: former head football coach at Alabama State University and Southern University.

Annabelle Belmard: first black to perform as a principal player with the Deutsche Opera in Berlin, Germany.

Louis Castenell: dean of the University of Cincinnati's College of Education.

Marie V. McDemmond: first female president of Norfolk State University (NSU).

Gilbert Rochon: sixth president of Tuskegee University.

Alexis Herman: first African American US Secretary of Labor.

Ivan L. R. Lemelle: judge, serving as US Magistrate Judge of the District Court, New Orleans, LA.

Regina Benjamin: current US Surgeon General.

Todd Stroger: elected Cook County Board President.

Stephen W. Rochon: director of Executive Residence and chief usher at the White House.

Candice Stewart: first African American Miss Louisiana and also Miss Louisiana Teen USA.

ATHLETIC SPORTS ABBREVIATIONS OF HBCUs

AMC	-	American Mideast Conference
NCAA	-	National Collegiate Athletic Association
NJCAA	-	National Junior Collegiate Athletic Association
ACCC	-	Alabama Community College Conference
NAIA	-	National Association of Intercollegiate Athletics
GCAC	-	Gulf Coast Athletic Conference
FCS	-	Football Championship Subdivision
MEAC	-	Mid-eastern Athletic Conference
CSFL	-	Central States Football League
CIAA	-	Central Intercollegiate Athletic Conference
RRAC	-	Red River Athletic Conference
MEC	-	Mountain East Conference
SWAC	-	Southwestern Athletic Conference
USCAA	-	United States Collegiate Athletic Association
FSC	-	Florida Sun Conference
SAC	-	South Atlantic Conference
SIAC	-	Southern Intercollegiate Athletic Conference
ACCC	-	Alabama Community College Conference
CSFL	-	Central States Football League
WVIA	-	West Virginia Intercollegiate Athletic Association
ECAC	-	Eastern College Athletic Conference
GLFC	-	Great Lakes Football Conference

CPSIA information can be obtained
at www.ICGtesting.com
Printed in the USA
LVHW041313300119
605791LV00001B/104